MW01010192

© 2013 *Kinfolk Magazine*

All rights reserved. No part of this publication
may be reproduced, distributed or transmitted
in any form or by any means, including pho-
tocopying or other electronic or mechanical
methods, without the prior written permission of the editor, except in the case of brief
quotations embodied in critical reviews and
certain other noncommercial uses permitted
by copyright law. For permission requests,
write to the editor, addressed "Attention:
Kinfolk Permissions," at the address below.

info@kinfolk.com
www.kinfolk.com

Kinfolk Magazine
328 NE Failing Street
Portland, Oregon 97212
Telephone: 503-946-8400
www.kinfolk.com

Printed in Canada

Publication Design by Amanda Jane Jones
Cover Photograph by Hideaki Hamada

KINFOLK

SUBSCRIBE

VISIT WWW.KINFOLK.COM/SUBSCRIBE

FOUR ISSUES EACH YEAR

CONTACT US

If you have any questions or comments,
email us at *info@kinfolk.com*

SUBSCRIPTIONS

For questions regarding your subscription,
email us at *subscribe@kinfolk.com*

STOCKISTS

If you would like to carry *Kinfolk*,
email us at *distribution@kinfolk.com*

SUBMISSIONS

Send all submissions to
submissions@kinfolk.com

WWW.KINFOLK.COM

WELCOME

How do you define your weekend? Do weekends still exist? Does yours fall on Tuesday and Wednesday? Are you capable of unplugging from your phones and computers? Whether you're reveling in the great outdoors, doing some marathon baking or just lounging on the couch, this issue is our guide to striking the right balance and making the most of our well-earned days off. I feel like a phony working on this issue, as mine rarely look like the chilled-out pages that follow. Like many of you, I often spend them typing away or working on a project. We all try to find rewarding work that makes our lives feel full, but our passion can be as dangerously all-consuming as it is wonderfully energizing.

Through our reader surveys, we learned that many of you are creative—students, photographers, designers, editors or small-business owners—which makes us wonder if you also have leisure-less weekends, hunched over your desk, with blurry boundaries between your work and off-hours. Keeping this in mind, we decided to dig deep on the subject of weekends and leisure to re-learn how to do nothing (The Idler, page 32), live more adventurously (The Lone Wolf Weekend, page 36) and embrace those two days, which are meant equally for rejuvenation and invigoration.

We came up with some practical tips for reversing hazardous work hours with our Weekend Workaholic Detox (page 30), and even share some harsh love with reminders on why you should exercise (The Water Within, page 24), but you may want to think twice before jogging through Manhattan on a busy Saturday (Saturday Slog, page 126). Our team found the most encouragement by hearing from inspiring artists and makers (Toast of the Town, page 54; Surf & Turf, page 66; The Milky Way, page 98) who have discovered their own ways to balance work, family, hobbies and downtime.

Take our Weekend issue, kick back, slip off your shoes and simply get out there and enjoy some good food and your favorite people.

NATHAN WILLIAMS, EDITOR OF KINFOLK MAGAZINE

NATHAN WILLIAMS
Editor
Portland, Oregon

AMANDA JANE JONES
Senior Designer
Chicago, Illinois

GAIL O'HARA
Copy Chief
Portland, Oregon

KATIE SEARLE-WILLIAMS
Web Editor
Portland, Oregon

DOUG BISCHOFF
Business Operations
Portland, Oregon

JOANNA HAN
Assistant Web Editor
Portland, Oregon

PAIGE BISCHOFF
Sales & Fulfillment
Portland, Oregon

JULIE POINTER
Gatherings
Portland, Oregon

ASIA RIKARD
Office Manager
Portland, Oregon

GEORGIA FRANCES KING
Writer & Editor
Brooklyn, New York

ANDREW & CARISSA GALLO
Filmmaker & Photographer
Portland, Oregon

MARÍA DEL MAR SACASA
Recipe Editor
New York, New York

SAKIKO SETAKA
Japan Assistant
Portland, Oregon

JODI MURPHY
Editorial Assistant
Portland, Oregon

TAYLOR STARK
Editorial Assistant
Portland, Oregon

ROMY ASH
Writer
Melbourne, Australia

LAUREN BAMFORD
Photographer
Melbourne, Australia

LOUISA THOMSEN BRITS
Writer
East Sussex, United Kingdom

ALISON BRISLIN
Stylist
Portland, Oregon

NILS BERNSTEIN
Writer
New York, New York

SARAH BURWASH
Illustrator
Nova Scotia, Canada

KAREL BALAS
Photographer
Paris, France

JAMES BOWDEN
Photographer
Bournemouth, United Kingdom

JUSTIN CHUNG
Photographer
New York, New York

LIZ CLAYTON
Writer
Brooklyn, New York

DAVID COGGINS
Writer
New York, New York

LAURA DART
Photographer
Portland, Oregon

MICHELLE DEBRUYN
Food Stylist
Seattle, Washington

DANNY DEMERS
Creative Director, Garçon Garçonne
Montreal, Canada

TINA MINAMI DHINGRA
Translator & Producer
Tokyo, Japan

PARKER FITZGERALD
Photographer
Portland, Oregon

MAIA FLORE
Photographer
Paris, France

NICOLE FRANZEN
Photographer
Brooklyn, New York

NEIL GAVIN
Photographer
New York, New York

ALICE GAO
Photographer
New York, New York

DIANE GARCIA
Creative Producer, Garçon Garçonne
Montreal, Canada

JIM GOLDEN
Photographer
Portland, Oregon

HIDEAKI HAMADA
Photographer
Osaka, Japan

AMY HEREFORD
Writer
Greenwood, Virginia

WILLIAM HEREFORD
Photographer
Brooklyn, New York

RUPERT LAMONTAGNE
Photographer
Montreal, Canada

NICHOLAS MCELROY
Photographer
Vancouver, Canada

RILEY MESSINA
Stylist
Portland, Oregon

SARAH MOROZ
Writer
Paris, France

OLIVIER RIELLAND NADEAU
Designer & Typographer
Montreal, Canada

MAJA NORRMAN
Photographer
Uppsala, Sweden

REBECCA PARKER PAYNE
Writer
Richmond, Virginia

LEO PATRONE
Photographer
Salt Lake City, Utah

NIKAELA MARIE PETERS
Writer
Winnipeg, Canada

CHRIS & SARAH RHOADS
Photographers & Directors
Seattle, Washington

LESLEY RIVERA
Photographer
Baltimore, Maryland

AUSTIN SAILSBURY
Writer
Copenhagen, Denmark

ANDERS SCHONNEMAN
Photographer
Copenhagen, Denmark

NATHALIE SCHWER
Stylist
Copenhagen, Denmark

KELSEY B. SNELL
Proofreader
Washington, D.C.

KATIE STRATTON
Painter
Dayton, Ohio

DAVID TANIS
Writer
New York, New York

SHOTA TASHIRO
Writer
Tokyo, Japan

SARAH TROTTER
Writer & Stylist
Melbourne, Australia

MICHELLE WONG
Prop Stylist
New York, New York

ONE

TWO

FEW

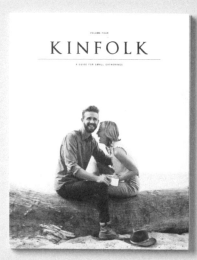

VOLUME FOUR

KINFOLK

A GUIDE FOR SMALL GATHERINGS

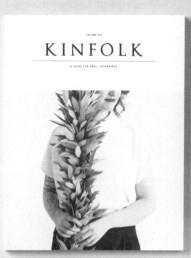

VOLUME SIX

KINFOLK

A GUIDE FOR SMALL GATHERINGS

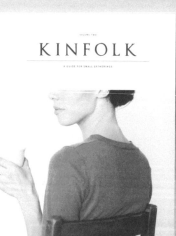

VOLUME TWO

KINFOLK

A GUIDE FOR SMALL GATHERINGS

VOLUME FIVE

KINFOLK

A GUIDE FOR SMALL GATHERINGS

SUBSCRIBE TO KINFOLK

We will mail you four issues per year:
$60 plus shipping & handling

Kinfolk is a quarterly, 144-page, ad-free print magazine that collects ideas from a growing international community of artists, writers, designers, photographers, cooks and others who are interested in creating small gatherings and finding new things to cook, make and do.

Printed in Canada on uncoated paper, each issue is filled with lush photography, lyrical essays, recipes, interviews, profiles, personal stories and practical tips along with a keen attention to design and details.

KINFOLK ONLINE PASS $40

· Using a Kinfolk Online Pass, you will be able to access stories from our back-issue archive and new stories from our current issue published gradually. (Back-issue stories are available via the web, not as downloadable PDFs.)

· Anyone visiting the site will be able to check out our new original web stories, City Guides, Films, Galleries and tons of beautiful images.

· The Kinfolk Online Pass is free with a print subscription or available separately.

· For more information, visit www.kinfolk.com/subscribe.

WWW.KINFOLK.COM

We launched a beautiful new website over the summer, which features fresh stories daily and content focusing on small gatherings and things to cook, make and do, including recipes, interviews and practical advice from our growing global community of foodie experts and friends.

Our freshly launched site also features our new *Kinfolk Saturdays* film series that offers adventurous ideas, inspiration and suggestions for ways to spend your weekend and our new City Guides section, which will highlight shops, restaurants and things to do that we love.

Get a Kinfolk Online Pass to access stories from our archive—it's free with a print subscription. Everyone can access our new original web stories, City Guides, Galleries and Films.

ONE

ENTERTAINING FOR ONE

○

KINGS & QUEENS: THE ART OF BED MAKING

Weekends provide a much-needed break from the monotony of the workweek—let this mean mornings when you don't just make your bed, you sculpt it.

A PHOTO ESSAY BY MAIA FLORE

Stay beneath the sheets all Saturday long. Be both the rafters and the resident of your own tepee.

Stack pillows high to turn a mattress into a chaise lounge—spend the afternoon comfortably propped up while reading or dreaming.

Center yourself on the bed and contort your body for a post-nap stretch.
Hold the position until sufficiently relaxed. Return to nap. ○

THE UTOPIAN FARMERS MARKET

Flannel, fennel and florals: How do you like your farmers markets? Are they clogged with strollers and totally cleaned out before you get there? Here's our guide to the way they should be.

WORDS BY GEORGIA FRANCES KING
ILLUSTRATION BY SARAH BURWASH

LOCATION Fields and parks may be sustenance for the soul, but they're also the preferred hunting grounds of mosquitos and irritable joggers. Fairs in elementary school parking lots may seem a little dystopian, but latent childhood memories lead to smiles, not to mention how basketball hoops provide perfect netting for macramé hanging planters.

CONVENIENCE So you can easily slog your stash home, markets situated within a bikeable distance are preferable for perusing. However, there's nothing more satisfying than taking a train, two buses and a short canoe ride to get to the lone place that sells your favorite homemade maple syrup. It's the modern equivalent of scavenging.

TIME There are two camps in the world of market timing: the gratification of bleary-eyed dawn forages as stall holders unpack their vans or the ease of a post-brunch rummage. The early birds may catch the best bunch of herbs, but they might also forget their wallets if leaving the house at 6 a.m. on a Sunday.

SERVICE When compared to supermarkets, understanding what you're putting in your gob is a definite tick in the farmers market box. Not only will the mustachioed fellow handing you a toothpick of home-cured salami be able to tell you what the hog ate for supper, he will encourage you to sneak the loose grapes too.

SELLERS From the calluses on their palms to the mild fragrance of compost, farmers can be surly folk. After all, if you were harvesting that much rhubarb on a weekly basis, you'd be a tad grumpy too. That's why it's often their younger, less world-weary sons and daughters who work the stalls with beaming country-life grins.

ATTENDEES The seasoned market aficionados can be spotted hauling their industrial trolleys from tent to tent, squeezing the avocados and fondling the strawberries. Their somewhat aggressive bartering manner may irk you (along with their wandering hands bruising the pears), but observe closely and you might pick up some haggling nuances.

DRESS CODE There is only one easy rule to obey in choosing the correct market attire: flannel. It's that simple. Along with a pair of goulash-encrusted jeans and leather lace-up boots, being precious about your slacks is not an alternative when towing around sacks of muddy turnips. Aprons, neck scarves and hairnets are optional.

FRESHNESS Checking for little creepy crawlies in celery hearts and scrubbing dirt-caked potatoes is a small price to pay for food-mile-free freshness. What goes home in your brown bag probably comes from a plantation a couple of miles down the road or—if you're cunning—off an overhanging peach branch across the street.

SIZE While supermarket fare comes in prepackaged sizes, market produce knows no magnitude. Whether it's teetering a squash the size of your head on your handlebars or purchasing a tiny jar of blackberry jam that you know you'll eat with a teaspoon instead of on toast, impractically sized food is a joy.

VARIETY While standard grocery items are pertinent to any dinner party, part of the fun of the farmers market is the popular game, "What the hell is that vegetable?" Zucchini the color of irises, kumquats the shape of crab apples, flowers that smell of cilantro–you're spoiled for choice in terms of unidentifiable goods.

PRESENTATION Faded wicker baskets, reclaimed oak benches and tin troughs once used for thirsty horses: wandering around a country market is the culinary equivalent of an antiques fair. Not only are the limes stacked in gravity-defying Jenga formations, but you might want to take a chomp out of the cedarwood stool they're sitting on too.

BAKED GOODS Pastries and chutneys abound! Even though your backpack may be stuffed with Granny Smiths and pecans to make a pie, you'll definitely need a little pre-made something to nosh on while you're waiting for the oven to preheat. It evens up that square meter of fresh kale you nabbed, too.

COFFEE QUEUE In the ultimate nirvana of markets, there would be enough coffee carts to supply the steady stream of caffeine-needing consumers. But we all know this is an inconceivable truth. Be sated waiting in line for freshly ground espresso by snooping in the trollies of the scroungers around you while planning your next move. ○

Georgia Frances King is an arts journalist who talks almost as much as she writes. Previously part of the frankie *magazine family in Melbourne, she has recently relocated to Brooklyn to scribble about cultural calamities from her little sun-filled flat in Greenpoint.*

ONE GOOD CHEF: DAVID TANIS

WORDS BY NILS BERNSTEIN & PHOTOS BY ALICE GAO

Former Chez Panisse chef and New York Times *food columnist David Tanis knows a whole lot about restaurant food, so why does he want us all to make food at home? We met with him in his East Village home to find out why serving your own simple creations is best.*

David Tanis wants you in the kitchen. Although he spent the better part of the past 30 years as co-head chef at Chez Panisse, his writing, including the weekly "City Kitchens" column in the *New York Times*, is meant to encourage people to cook at home, regardless of their real or perceived limitations. His first two cookbooks, *A Platter of Figs and Other Recipes* and *Heart of the Artichoke and Other Kitchen Journeys*, established him in the same motivational, garden-driven league as Nigel Slater and Yotam Ottolenghi. *One Good Dish*, published in October, puts forth the idea that one trustworthy dish can make—or even *be*—the meal. Its approachable recipes reflect both his family memories and global travels: Waffle-Iron Grilled Cheese, Lamb with Cumin, Mackerel Rillettes, Scallop *Tod Mun*, Charred Endives with Anchovy Butter, a deceptively simple garlic soup and even the European concept of watered-down wine. The book is as suited to cobbling dishes together for a dinner party as it is to making a leisurely, comforting dinner for one.

WHY *ONE GOOD DISH*?

Sometimes a meal doesn't have to be an orchestrated affair to be pleasing and to be satisfying. My thought was to pare it down to what makes a good eating experience, and sometimes it is just one good dish. Not that the book is about one-dish meals—though some of the dishes *are* one-dish meals—but that here is a dish that I know is going to be delicious, and that's enough.

ALL YOUR BOOKS HAVE A COMMON THREAD OF FINDING PLEASURE IN THE COOKING PROCESS, NOT JUST THE FINISHED DISH.

The whole idea is that it's not just about fuel. I want the experience at the table to be enjoyable, but I also want the experience of getting there to be enjoyable. Maybe it starts with going to the market and getting excited about the fact that tomatoes are ripe. And, you think, Well, that's lunch—lunch is a tomato sandwich.

There's been such a disconnect—so many people still don't know where food comes from or how it's grown or what's seasonal, even though there's increasing interest in it. Some people go to the farmers market to buy food, but many go for a window-shopping experience—the same way that people watch cooking shows but don't cook, they have a fancy kitchen but never use it.

My hope is that my books are user-friendly and actually do provide that inspiration, to give you permission to make something that you know how to make, remind you that you probably know more about cooking than you think you do, and maybe add a few more ideas.

WHAT DO YOU LIKE TO MAKE WHEN YOU ENTERTAIN?

My focus isn't on cooking to impress but cooking to please. Most people try to do too much. A rustic stew can be just as satisfying—or more so—than an expensive roast.

DO YOU HAVE ANY WEEKEND RITUALS, WHETHER AROUND FOOD OR ANYTHING ELSE?

Well, I will say that going out for brunch is *not* one of my weekend rituals! No disrespect for people that do. I understand the inclination to have a relaxing meal—your Eggs Benedict, your Bloody Mary—but when did it become set in stone that that's what a weekend meal was supposed to be? Rather than brunch, I really love a midday meal that goes on a few hours, slightly later in the day. The weekend is a time to do the things that you like, and a time to relax, and one of the things that I like to do is make something to eat. I find it relaxing to make it, and I find it relaxing to have people join.

HOW HAS FINDING THAT BALANCE CHANGED FROM WHEN YOU WERE IN A RESTAURANT KITCHEN ALL WEEK?

I don't think my focus has shifted that much. Even working late nights in the restaurant, I would always cook something when I got home. The staff would have a meal, but to me, it was too close to the action. I couldn't relax with a meal when I was in work mode, so most nights I would come home at 11 or midnight and make something to eat. It gets to some of the things in this book, like making garlic toast. Add a glass of wine, maybe a piece of cheese and a couple slices of prosciutto and you're having a very nice meal—and you didn't pick up a bad pizza on the way home just because you're starving.

WHAT ARE SOME OTHER THINGS YOU LIKE TO MAKE JUST FOR YOURSELF?

I like the idea of making yourself a delicious pasta. A lot of times making pasta for more than two people can be tricky; for instance, Pasta Carbonara—you can't make it for six people. There are a lot of dishes that are actually better for one. And I really like to make a small amount of soup.

CHEZ PANISSE HAS ALWAYS BEEN AT THE CENTER OF PROMOTING SOCIAL AND ENVIRONMENTAL AWARENESS THROUGH FOOD. WHAT ARE SOME THINGS A HOME COOK CAN DO?

There is the whole "vote with your fork" idea, and it's true. Support people who are actually taking the care to grow vegetables properly, without pesticides, and know that the large Monsanto-type corporations aren't interested in the earth or environment or anyone's longevity. It's a long story, and Michael Pollan has a lot of great things to say about it, but basically if it doesn't look like food, don't eat it. People need to do the best they can, but also to understand that you can't depend on big companies to nourish you. You have to nourish your people and nourish yourself. o

Nils Bernstein works by day as a music publicist for one of America's finest indie labels. His writing has appeared in Bon Appétit, Men's Journal *and* Wine Enthusiast. *He lives in New York but escapes to Mexico City every chance he gets.*

See David's Niçoise Salad on a Roll recipe on page 137.

THE LANGUAGE OF SWIMMING

WORDS BY NIKAELA MARIE PETERS & PHOTOGRAPHS BY LAURA DART

*Once you learn it, you will always remember how to communicate
with the water. The movement is etched in your brain. The moment
rejuvenates the soul. Swim, just swim.*

S wimming is like riding a bike. Once it is in your neurological pathways, the ability to swim stays with you, an inoculation against drowning.

Swimming is like a first language. It may be years between swims. You may be out of breath, herky-jerky and graceless—but you won't drown after not doing it for years. You'll remember how to communicate with the water. You'll feel the water encompassing your body, and then—like a piece of clothing—you won't feel it at all.

You'll tip your head back and float, lazy as a muskrat. You might notice the warbling voices of your swim-mates through the water, perhaps a distant boat or the splash of a cannonball (the human kind). The sun is warm on your face and you kick, twist and dive. It makes you feel like you are six years old again, and you open your eyes in the greeny gloom and smile and then look for an unsuspecting leg to grab.

There's the smell of the color green. In the pre-dawn gray, a figure moves. A sound between a slap and a knock breaks the stillness—bare feet on wood, and then a larghetto *pat pat pat pat pat*—until the sudden accelerando, a brief pause and… splash: an imperfect dive off the dock. The loons ask questions. The evidence: a discarded towel and ripples multiplying like tree rings on the otherwise unbroken surface of the lake, marking off the seconds until the next breath.

The diver-cum-swimmer reemerges in a flash of glistening skin, quickening heartbeat, contained alarm. Four strokes and a turn. Two hands on the ladder. And out she comes, like Naaman from the Jordan, clean.

––––––––

The first time a prairie kid sees the ocean is the first time she gets a true sense of the bigness of the world and her own smallness in it. The infinite horizon. The nonstop crash crash crash.

After hopscotching on hot sand to the water's edge, spent waves tear the ground from beneath your feet as they recede. It's a slow, cautious progress from feet to ankles to knees to waist to diving in headfirst. This is a new kind of swimming. Far from chlorine pool lessons, it feels like a soft form of survival, a kind of prayer. A tiny being in the boisterous arms of Infinity.

Salty skin, red eyes, blue lips, chattering teeth, thunder-clapping waves, screaming laughter: joy. And later, the best feeling of tired. ○

Nikaela Marie Peters lives in Winnipeg, Manitoba, Canada. She is currently completing graduate studies in theology. The photographs for this story were taken in Tivoli, New York.

THE WATER WITHIN

WORDS BY GAIL O'HARA & PHOTOGRAPH BY JIM GOLDEN

Sweating has some negative connotations, but we all do it and it is actually a pretty essential bodily function. Here is a list of ways to get sweaty and reasons why you should.

When you consider that sweat is mainly composed of water and salt, it's not such a bad thing. The benefits of sweating are plenty: It makes you cool, lowers your heart rate and makes your skin clear. It protects you from evil—well, it contains an antimicrobial protein that helps to stave off infection. It helps us communicate our emotions to others (for better or worse). It aids in proper blood flow and brings oxygen to the skin, and research has proven that it's one of the most effective stress relievers on the planet. We advocate the act of sweating, as it means you are out there doing some stuff, keeping things moving, and you'll be happier, foxier and more relaxed as a result. We made a list of good ways to get a little bit sweaty.

1. Take your dog (Steinbeck? Julian? Fido?) to the dog park and get moving. Watch your step.

2. Get into a furiously competitive game of ping-pong with some under-12s. Or your roommates.

3. Join a bicycle gang. Please, no Lycra.

4. Get a mini trampoline, put on some pulsing disco and bounce.

5. Climb trees. Climb a mountain. Just climb, dammit.

6. Simple Frisbee (no hacky sack please).

7. Put on some 1980s dance-pop like New Order and dance madly in your living room.

8. Do some aqua aerobics or just jump in a lake.

9. Skateboard across town. Try to resist grabbing the back of a truck.

10. Spend time wrestling with your favorite human or animal.

11. Chase small children around a muddy field: They cannot get enough.

12. Get your jump ropes out and play with the neighborhood kids.

13. Channel your inner Beckham: Join an amateur soccer league. ○

Gail O'Hara is the copy chief at Kinfolk. *She also runs* chickfactor.

PHOTO ESSAY

WEEKEND INDULGENCES

Weekends are a time for comfort and relaxing and maybe rewarding yourself a little. Are there treats that you only allow yourself on weekends? We asked our friends and contributors what food and drink items make them weak in the knees.

PHOTOGRAPHS BY JIM GOLDEN

TOP SHELF: Olive & Sinclair Chocolate Co. (*oliveandsinclair.com*), crackers & cheese, Fentimans Dandelion & Burdock soda (*fentimans.com*), Pixie Retreat raw chocolates (*pixieretreat.com*), Morris Kitchen Preserved Lemon Syrup (*morriskitchen.com*), Jacobsen Salt Co. Oregon Pinot Noir Flake Salt (*jacobsensalt.com*), Jack Rudy Cocktail Co. gin & tonic (*jackrudycocktailco.com*), lemon cream tart (*wholefoodsmarket.com*)

BOTTOM SHELF: Pacific Northwest Cilantro Lime and Jalapeño Kale Chips (*pacifickale.com*), roasted red peppers, barbecued corn, a glass of good red wine, chanterelle mushrooms, Taza Cacao Puro Mexican chocolate (*tazachocolate.com*), rosemary-brown sugar popcorn, Basil Hayden's bourbon (*basilhaydens.com*), Jacques Torres Chocolate Chip Cookies (*mrchocolate.com*), Woodblock Chocolate (*woodblockchocolate.com*), Pocky (*pocky.glico.com*)

TOP SHELF: Key lime and fresh fruit tarts, Siggi's yogurt (*skyr.com*), Elizabethan Pantry Lemon Curd, Buddha's Tears Tea (*townshendstea.com*), dried mango slices, Bellocq Tea Atelier Chai Tea (*bellocq.com*), chocolate brittle, Big Spoon Roasters Peanut Cocoa (*bigspoonroasters.com*), Sweet Deliverance NYC Apple Raisin Chili Chutney (*sweetdeliverancenyc.com*), baguettes from a local bakery

BOTTOM SHELF: Ines Rosales Seville Orange Tortas (*inesrosalesusa.com*), Heart coffee (*heartroasters.com*), Olive & Sinclair Chocolate Co. (*oliveandsinclair.com*), Cowgirl Creamery cheeses (*cowgirlcreamery.com*), Olympic Provisions salami (*olympicprovisions.com*), Vecchia Modena Lambrusco, chocolate-covered almonds, freshly squeezed orange juice ○

THE WEEKEND WORKAHOLIC DETOX

WORDS BY GEORGIA FRANCES KING

Do you work a full week and then spend the whole weekend obsessing over your in-box too? Use our handy seven-step guide to stepping away from the computer and taking back your weekend.

It's Saturday morning. While your friends are devouring poached eggs drenched in hollandaise at the café around the corner, you're staring into the black hole of your laptop screen clutching a to-go cup of lukewarm brew. And you're not the only one foregoing fresh bagels instead of website cookies. You, like many other stay-at-home creatives, have a problem. You're a WWW: a Wired Weekend Workaholic. When the line between work and play is as blurry as your 1 a.m. computer vision, it can be tough to switch your brain off and give it some rest. That's where we come in. Step away from your computer. Go for a run around the block. Give us five reasons why it can't wait until Monday. Here is our seven-step detox for the weekend workaholic.

—

STEP 1: SWITCH OFF, LITERALLY Come the weekend, if you find yourself pulling your phone away from the grips of others screaming, "JUST ONE MORE E-MAIL," it might be time to disconnect. So you're not sneaking peeks of your in-box on your phone, here's the best way to avoid temptation: Go find your modem. Now yank out its power supply. And don't plug it back in until Monday morning at 9 a.m. To help, perhaps draw a frowny face on a Post-it Note and stick it on there, or get someone to hide it from you in the house (just don't go looking for it in a neurotic game of hide-and-seek). As you are now connectionless, this might mean you have to plan a little ahead—pre-download whatever movies you want to watch, work out directions to dinner and forecast the weather beforehand. Otherwise there are these amazing things called video stores, maps and barometers—you might have heard of them.

STEP 2: MAKE A LIST Was your to-do list becoming as long as the memo of cities Napoleon wanted to conquer? Try making a non-work-related list of things you'd like to achieve this weekend. Now tick them off with the same zest you would a mammoth work time line. Such activities could include errands, people you want to see, recipes you want to try or attempting to drink a whole cup of tea without any other distractions. Another great list-related practice to fool yourself into doing some personal work is writing down a dozen simple undertakings that make you feel good: calling your mom, making your bed with fresh sheets, walking in the rain or drinking piña coladas. Try to do one of these every day and you'll feel like you're achieving something outside of a deadline.

STEP 3: RELAX. OR AT LEAST TRY TO Pacing up and down your hallway and sternly telling yourself to relax is about as calming as climbing spike walls or dining with your in-laws. It's the unfortunate double-edged sword of working from home that, when faced with a pressing deadline, you'll find yourself staring wistfully into your fridge every 20 minutes. But when you're endeavoring to rest, that's when the motivation hits to pump out another thousand words. If you stop trying to force yourself into unwinding, it'll eventually come along and swaddle you in its cushioned, chamomile-scented arms. To help it along, attempt to reset your brain to feel accomplishment from doing homely things like growing orchids or finishing *Anna Karenina*, not handing in deadlines.

STEP 4: DO THINGS THAT ARE IMPRACTICAL TO TECHNOLOGY There's one natural element that computers, cameras, notepads and conference calls despise: water. Draw yourself a long hot bath, grab a book off your library shelf and stay in there until your toes are pruned and the water is cool. Head to your local pool with a bag of cherries in the warmer weather, or take a trek out to a nearby lake or waterway for a paddle. Long walks and hikes will also put some distance between you and your laptop—just don't "accidentally" walk into a café with free Wi-Fi. You're not fooling anyone.

STEP 5: TRICK YOURSELF INTO STASIS If you're really struggling to unhook yourself from your in-box (it's 8 a.m. on a Sunday—no one is going to e-mail you aside from rich Nigerian princesses), you should try getting hooked on something else. Introducing the DVD box set. Try to pick a TV show with as many cliff-hangers as possible so you'll be timing light-speed toilet breaks instead of disinterestedly reaching for your sketch pad between episodes. However, avoid watching anything that might act as a trigger for your guilt factor. So if you're in the public service, don't watch *The West Wing*. If you're a creative director, then no *Mad Men* for you. And bootleggers shouldn't watch *Boardwalk Empire* for the same reason motorcycle gang members should stay away from *Sons of Anarchy*.

STEP 6: BE REALISTIC Creating improbable expectations of workless weekends is only going to leave you feeling anxious and upset if you fail. So be realistic. And don't kid yourself: Working from the couch is still working, even if you're in your pajamas and the midday movie is rustling in the background. When there's a particularly nasty deadline around the corner, try not to be dismayed when you find yourself retreating back to your computer. After all, we're only human. But if you really need to get something done (and we mean *really*), make sure it happens on the sofa.

STEP 7: REWARD YOURSELF Whew. That was hard, right? You've maintained some self-control, rejuvenated your brain cells and achieved sweet, sweet nothing workwise this weekend. Congratulations! And good behavior shouldn't go uncompensated. Buy yourself a fancy French treat, pour yourself a glass of wine or take yourself out to dinner. Just don't reward yourself with a respite-filled glimpse at that PowerPoint presentation. At least not till Monday. ○

THE IDLER

As people get older, they realize that time is more valuable than money. And finding more time to do absolutely nothing is perhaps exactly what we all need.

WORDS BY NIKAELA MARIE PETERS
PHOTOGRAPHS BY MAJA NORRMAN

It's the stuff of gods and infants—the birthplace of great works of art, philosophy and science. The habit of doing nothing at all is super-important to our individual and cultural well-being, yet it seems to be dying in our digitized age.

Far from laziness, proper idleness is the soul's home base. Before we plan or love or decide or act or storytell, we are idle. Before we learn, we watch. Before we do, we dream. Before we play, we imagine. The idle mind is awake but unconstrained, free to slip untethered from idea to idea or meander from potential theory to potential truth. Thomas Aquinas argued that "it is necessary for the perfection of human society that there should be men who devote their lives to contemplation."

Is true idleness a lost skill? How often do we sit, serenely unoccupied? How often do we walk, as Henry David Thoreau advised, with no agenda or destination, present and free? What an uncommon sight: a solitary individual, his head not buried in a newspaper or laptop or phone, simply sitting—his mind long wandered off.

Seven years ago, I lived in an apartment without an Internet connection. I had a flip cell phone that only worked to make calls and send 40-character texts. Without the distraction of the Internet or the option of watching a movie,

I was certainly more productive, according to certain measures. A mind adrift in a sea of its own making is far more interesting than a mind following a trail of hyperlinks. But what strikes me as a greater loss—when I compare those years to now—is all the time I spent doing "nothing." My bedroom had a third-story view of a busy downtown street. It was small, and the bed was pushed up against the window. I'm sure the hours I spent staring out that window would add up to weeks of time. I watched nothing and anything. I (occasionally) smoked cigarettes and drank coffee… two habits that, while unhealthy for the body, do—in certain circumstances—

have health benefits for the soul.

Productivity is not the only measure of time well spent. Some of the most important scientific innovations and inventions were "happened upon," unplanned, after years of unproductive, leisurely puzzling. My five-month-old understands this intuitively. He will learn an entire language and how to sit, stand, crawl and walk all mostly by doing what, to an adult, would look like "nothing."

I'm convinced that time spent idle makes for a healthier state of mind. We want less and are more at peace when we get it. We sleep better and work harder. Simpler things bring us joy. When

we daily observe our immediate surroundings, we are more grounded in our context, more attuned to the rhythms of whatever season or place we are in.

Plus, the changing shapes of clouds need our attention. ○

THE ART OF DAYTIME DRINKING

WORDS BY DAVID COGGINS & PHOTOGRAPH BY NICOLE FRANZEN

Whether you're at a wedding, a friend's birthday soirée or just catching up on e-mails, sometimes the weekend involves a fair bit of daytime drinking. Here's our clear-headed guide to spending the day with an open bottle.

When you leave the farmers market on a Saturday morning—after wondering where all your cash went—you are in the mood to prepare your microgreens, your heritage pork chops, your Hen of the Woods mushrooms and finish perhaps with some Vermont cheese made by Middlebury dropouts. You look forward to the specific pleasure of preparing food picked that day, food that has never seen the inside of a refrigerator. You feel virtuous, you feel hungry.

Along with your feast, your good afternoon might involve an English soccer game in the background, some writing, catching up on a week's worth of newspapers and the occasional visitor bearing still more food. But most importantly, you deserve a glass of wine. Better than that, you deserve a bottle. Not a default bottle sitting around, but a good bottle, something worth considering. But you want to balance your pleasures, not pass out by 4 in the afternoon. There are some tactics for the advanced daytime drinking, which really is a worthwhile pursuit.

Let's discuss our terms. You've graduated from Bloody Marys in bars. We've all been there, but it's getting harder to do. In Manhattan, at least, heading out after 11 in the morning is dangerous business. Brunch is a depraved battlefield. It's trench warfare you can't win—unless you abstain. Consider yourself a conscientious objector. Although the Ear Inn at opening time is not a bad place to sort it out. It's an old bar on Spring Street, very far west, almost at the water, with a nautical theme (before there were themes). It's a classic, but the type of place where you know better than to order too ambitiously.

We've spent time drinking very cold martinis in the sunshine at exactly 5 in the afternoon. It's a fine pleasure, but martinis are a commitment, and two of them set you down a path that bends back to sobriety very slowly. So we focus on a more viable, more versatile approach. For those who desire to drink with an eye toward the end of the day, we have one word for you: Riesling.

Riesling is easy drinking in the best sense (as opposed to light beer, which is an alternate to water best suited to a day on a Montana trout stream). It's often low in alcohol content (it's not hard to find a good bottle less than 10 percent, others are less than 8 percent). One pivotal fact about Riesling: It doesn't have to be sweet. In fact, the preference here is for those without residual sugar, which, as a critic would say, are bracingly acidic. It's a grape with a clarity unlike any other, a sunniness with no humidity. It's refined without being precious—it's clean and direct. There's also something psychological about the shape of a Riesling bottle—it's so slender and understated—that makes you feel like you haven't done anything too drastic.

So, what happens in the winter months? I'm glad you asked. If you want to strike fear into your more delicate friends, serve them a Bull Shot (think of it as a Bloody Mary with beef bouillon instead of tomato juice). That will get their attention. Otherwise, you have to make some heavy decisions to make. Full-bodied wines taste so much better with food: If you open one as you begin your prep work than you've got to tread lightly. Our preference is for a good light red Burgundy during prep. If it manages to disappear, then you graduate to a Rhône for lunch. At this point, you should be so lucid that doing the *New York Times* acrostic should be no problem at all. ○

David Coggins is a writer and editor who follows Kingsley Amis' advice to "drink wine in quantity." His work has appeared in Esquire, Art in America *and* Interview. *He lives in New York.*

THE LONE WOLF WEEKEND

When most people think of camping, they think about doing it with friends or family. But camping alone can be exactly what you need to turn inward, look outward and revel in the quiet.

PHOTO ESSAY BY JAMES BOWDEN

*James Bowden (pictured above) is a freelance photographer and surfer based
either on the south coast of England or in Hobart, Tasmania. This photo
essay was shot by James alone at a secret spot somewhere in the southwest of
England. James bolted for the weekend, grabbed a few surfboards and camped
out at a rare quiet spot.*

TWO

ENTERTAINING FOR TWO

○ ○

NEIGHBORS: A BLESSED BURDEN

WORDS BY NIKAELA MARIE PETERS & PHOTOGRAPH BY LESLEY RIVERA

We choose our friends and we are born into our families, but neighbors are just randomly assigned. Nikaela Marie Peters explores the complex relationship we have with those who live in the next room.

Inside our singular personalities live two opposing characters: the extrovert and the hermit. Negotiating the tension between the two is a burden, but it's a burden that makes us human. The Internet has recently allowed us the option of resolving this tension. Online, the recluse can commune, and the extrovert can hide. The Internet seduces us, leading us to believe that we author our identities. We decide what to share and determine how others will see us. We're effectively freed from the confines of time and place.

In truth though, our identities are not fixed, but fluid: formed by our relationships, contexts, histories and homes—our time and place. Living in a time and a place means having neighbors: Noisy, nosy, occasionally delightful people who encroach on our lives and parking spots and affect us in both meaningful and trivial ways. They know things we do not necessarily choose to share with them: which newspaper we get delivered, the contents of our recycling bins, what time we turn our lights out at night and that we leave our Christmas tree on our porch until April. Neighbors become some of the most important relationships we have because they keep the extrovert-hermit tension alive. We feel burdened because we desire to both hide from—and open our doors to—them.

I remember many neighbors. Once as a kid, my family and I listened from our tent as the woman and man in the campsite next to ours fought. They yelled at each other long into the night. We felt sad for them. In the morning, the woman and the camper trailer were gone. The man was sitting alone on a lawn chair next to a clump of evergreens, watching a tiny TV with rabbit ears plugged into the campsite outlet.

In my first apartment downtown, the door next to mine opened into a windowless apartment occupied by a quiet German man. He collected old wheelchairs, rode his bicycle in winter and listened to cassette-tape sermons loud enough for me to hear. At least once a month, he cleaned his apartment, setting all of his belongings out in the hallway to make room to vacuum.

In the house next to the one I grew up in lived a woman who used an umbrella only on the sunniest days.

A man who set the building on fire because he forgot to turn off the coffee maker occupied the apartment above my best friends' place.

The landlord of my last apartment always finished a conversation saying, in his Serbian accent, "We gonna see each other." And he was right. We always saw each other.

That's what makes neighbors neighbors: They see each other. We don't choose them. We can't control how they see us. We're blessed with the real, physical, challenge of living with and beside other human beings. There's no such thing as a digital neighbor. Online, we can make friends, but we don't have neighbors. Neighbors are necessarily physical. And this is why they're important. They soften our edges. They keep us human. They're given to us instead of chosen by us; they teach us grace. ○○

TWO'S A CROWD: TIPS FOR TRAVELING DUOS

WORDS BY GEORGIA FRANCES KING & PHOTOGRAPHS BY MAIA FLORE

Weekend trips for two conjure images of candlelit dinners and screaming matches from passenger-seat drivers. We have a few suggestions for getting through a romantic getaway unscathed.

If a few simple rules aren't taken into account, romantic getaways for two can easily turn into real-time repeats of *The Shining*. Here's your quick-fire guide to traveling with your significant other without breaking up.

1. A successful non-throat-throttling holiday starts before you even lock the back door. Pack and prepare everything well ahead of time to ensure that passports are secured and Wellies have been located, otherwise you might not make it to the end of the block without strangling each other.

2. Complimentary bottles of hotel wine can do wonders for jet lag but not your nasal passages. If you find yourself constantly waking to ceaseless snoring, build a pillow fort barrier around your ears instead of attacking your snotty partner—this will only lead to resentment and a room fluffy with goose down.

3. Even if you normally bunk with your special someone nightly back home, one of the key advantages of hotel-size king mattresses is being able to starfish your limbs in every direction. To be the nice one, suck it up, roll to the edge and allow your partner that small joy.

4. Organize your morning bathroom schedule the night before to avoid cold showers and cold shoulders. Everyone needs their morning alone time. Think of your trip as pizza dough: It's best to leave it to rise alone, as otherwise you'll be left feeling dissatisfied and oddly hungry.

5. Never, ever fight about directions, unless that direction is about to send you careening off a rocky cliff face. You can always turn around, have a cup of roadside tea and retrace your steps or—God forbid—ask for directions.

6. Find the importance of alone time. Not only do you want an escape from the banality of regular life, but also possibly from each other. Even if it's just a morning constitutional around the motel parking lot or offering to fetch bitter coffees, spend a little time solo every day.

7. Holidays are meant for getting out of your humdrum routine and experiencing something new, and that doesn't mean falling into your same couchy habits in a different city. If you find yourself repeating your old ways of bedside *Twin Peaks* marathons, then nudge each other until you're outside of your collective comfort zones.

8. Learn how to compromise on the little things by meeting in the middle: So they want the cheese platter and you're keen on the lemon cake? Settle on the cheesecake (or just get both—you're on holiday, after all). ○○

STAYCATIONS: A HOLIDAY AT HOME

WORDS BY GEORGIA FRANCES KING

While everyone else competes for limited highway space this weekend, why not just turn your home into the ideal space for a dream staycation? Here's our guide to vacationing without opening your wallet or car door.

Times may be a tad tough, but finding time is even tougher. If you're struggling to grab more than a few days off or ruffling among the couch cushions for loose change, here is a word that might be handy for you: staycation. No bedbug-infested hotel rooms, no knee-cramping flights, no slimy travel agents—just you, your abode and your stay-at-home vacation. The trick is to fool yourself into feeling like you've been transported into a nostalgic wonderland, not the other end of your living room. While pillow forts will never grow old as long as there's a bottle of Shiraz involved, here are a few ideas for grown-up staycations that bring a new meaning to "home away from home."

BREAK ROUTINE The first step to a successful staycation is eradicating your daily habits and re-creating the types you might form if waking up to a Mai Tai and a foot rub every day. Granola may be a hassle-free breakfast option, but try preparing yourself a fully cooked brunch in bed each morning (better yet, get someone else to make it for you). After making your bed, put a comically sized chocolate on your pillow for you to miraculously find later in the day. Only wash using individual gourmet soaps. Even fold your toilet paper down into those nifty little triangles. By tricking yourself into thinking you're not at home, you'll be less likely to start pottering about and sorting your sock cupboard.

EAT OUT You know that little Italian joint around the corner? The one with the gingham tablecloths that look like Dorothy got lost on her way to Oz? The one you never normally go to because you figure you can make pasta at home? Go there. But not just in your slacks and T-shirt—get dressed up. Be the best-dressed person in that tiny trattoria, just short of wearing a full-length ball gown. Order a bottle of Chianti. Bring your own candles. Reenact scenes from *Lady and the Tramp*. Making the familiar seem exotic is a staycation must.

OR, EAT IN Some recipes require several days and a whole lot of patience to bring into fruition. That's several successive days you don't typically possess to spend in the kitchen with your forearms in several ounces of dough. So have a whirl at curing your own meat or fish. Soak a variety of dry beans. Make your own puff pastry. Take some time to master the processes your grandparents used from scratch, and enjoy the lengthy method instead of attempting to speed it up. If you want to take your culinary holiday to the next level, get creative and theme every day's meals around a different concept—like a country or a color—and only munch on foodstuffs relating to that notion.

GET OUT OF TOWN Getting out of the house for a sojourn is a fine way to stave off staycation cabin fever. Take yourself on a day trip (just not the type the Beatles sung about) by finding a quaint place a few hours out of town, packing a picnic lunch and pioneering your own surroundings. A definite advantage of day trips is that you get to go home at sundown, not find a dodgy roadside motel with more flickering neon lights than an early-'90s rave. Go fruit picking, visit a distant cookie-bearing relative or set out to spend five bucks in every thrift shop within a five-mile radius. Head to the tourist spot you always felt too silly to visit and force yourself to take the cheesiest photograph possible. To make your day-holiday feel authentic, send your friend a postcard, even if it's just from the pub two towns over. And the best, cockle-warming part? By staying close to home, you're revitalizing local small business owners. High-fives all around.

OR, STAY IN If you don't desire to take off your pajamas all day, there are plenty of ways to transform your home into a resort with its own activity schedule. If you have a balcony or backyard, then buy a blow-up pool and invite some buddies around for a paddle. Search the cupboards for a dusty Trivial Pursuit set and have a game night. Create a bowling alley in your hallway using toilet rolls and a tennis ball. Source an old projector and a sheet, and set up your own indoor cinema complete with salted caramel popcorn. The biggest rule is trying not to do anything you'd perform on an average weekend, otherwise you'll go back to the daily grind feeling like you've wasted your staycation attempting to resist cleaning the gutters. That means no *Seinfeld* marathons, no vacuuming and no standing in front of the fridge eating peanut butter with a spoon. Well, at least not every day. ○ ○

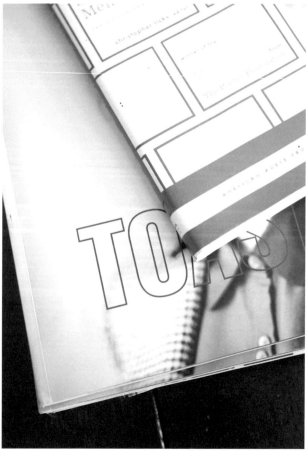

TOAST OF THE TOWN

WORDS BY LOUISA THOMSEN BRITS & PHOTOGRAPHS BY NEIL GAVIN

How does a creative power couple like James and Jessica Seaton, founders of the British clothing and home goods company Toast, find a balance between work and play? We chatted with them over coffee at a London café about how they manage to stay grounded.

Back in 1997, Jessica and James Seaton started a small business selling pajamas out of their farmhouse in the Welsh countryside. Some 16 years later, their clothing and home goods company is an enduring symbol of quality that manages to be both classic and modern. Toast publishes a beautifully styled mail-order catalog, and its products are available in some boutiques around the United Kingdom (toast.co.uk), as well as at Selfridges.

In the UK, a piece of toast represents comfort. Eating toast is a simple, easygoing, almost symbolic thing—a slice of home snatched and buttered on the way out the door or something more wholesome enjoyed on slow mornings, served with jam or smoked salmon or with a boiled egg. The Toast company seems to have been crafted from moments like these—it's a seductive combination of honesty, poetry and practicality sprung from the kind of relaxed dialogue, possibility and easy flow of a weekend morning. We caught up with the pair behind Toast to find out about their work-life balance.

HOW EASY IS IT FOR YOU TO STAY TRUE TO THE SPIRIT OF SIMPLE PLEASURE CAPTURED IN THE PAGES OF A TOAST CATALOG?

Jessica: A piece of toast is a humble thing. We'd like to think that Toast is accessible and democratic, right from the name. Everything we do should resonate with that somehow.

James: When you start a business, it's like riding a bike, easy and responsive. Now it's a lorry [truck]. I know what it has to be and keep that in mind. It's about authenticity. It requires a different way of being. Sometimes the right thing to do commercially is not the right thing for Toast. Toast isn't offering something unrealistic. It's attainable. It's absolutely possible for most of us to take a short walk or just to go to a quiet part of the house with a book and read.

Jessica: Toast is about groundedness. It was always about more than clothes and bed linen. Village life grounds us, and it epitomizes that democratic thing. You make friends with everybody—good behavior is bound by shared values. I adore village hall teas.

At weekends, at home in the village, we walk, we catch up with ourselves and the maintenance of things. We prepare food, eat together and garden. Well, I garden. Mostly in the vegetable patch—we have fruit trees establishing themselves. We're training pear cordons, have had little success with asparagus, are fighting off gooseberry sawfly, growing raspberries, currants, blueberries and artichokes. It's a full-array vegetable garden.

IS THAT WHERE YOU REALLY UNWIND?

Jessica: I'm quite driven deep down. I'm keen on doing things. I love getting out into the garden—I love the feeling of the earth. My drive for perfection can sometimes overwhelm the release gained by the outdoors, the connection with plants and the feel and smell of the soil. But it's certainly lovely to walk out to gather some herbs, a cabbage or such for supper at the end of a long day. Rudyard Kipling's poem "The Camel's Hump" captures the release from the tyranny of your own head, which can sometimes be gained from throwing oneself into a simple physical task.

James: You only need small refreshing moments to top up your sense of how well everything is. At the moment in Swansea, there is a suspendedness and wonderfulness. All you need is to step out for five minutes to top it up. If your actions don't have that stuff as fuel, they are just actions. I suppose the fuel is a sense of wonder.

It's very important to have time to stop and stare. I go for walks, cycle and I love swimming in wild water. I used to keep bees. I would lie in the long grass, by the hives, having them land on my finger, listening to them. I'm more contemplative—or lazy maybe. I bore very easily. Something will catch my interest or not at all. I like subverting customary ways of thinking.

Jessica: Thinking can so often run along established tracks. Someone to rock the boat is invaluable.

IS THAT WHY YOU BUILT A GARDEN SHED INSIDE YOUR LONDON OFFICE, AS A PLACE TO THINK, TO RETREAT TO?

James: We built a shed because the office is steel and glass and modern, and I wanted to subvert that. It didn't cost any more to build a shed.

Jessica: You have a love-hate relationship with your shed.

James: I have a love-hate relationship with work.

HAS THE WAY TECHNOLOGY SEEPS INTO EVERYDAY LIFE MADE IT DIFFICULT TO DRAW A LINE BETWEEN WORK AND HOME?

Jessica: Life has become increasingly fast-paced. The connectivity means the boundaries between work and non-work and relaxation are more smudgy. We have to impose them ourselves. We need to acknowledge the importance of establishing boundaries on other people's ability to call on our time. I suppose it's about balancing risk and opportunity. Connectivity allows you to be engaged with work in a productive way while living the life you need to live. When we first moved to Swansea, we had to drive 20 miles to the nearest library to find an encyclopedia. Now we can stay in touch on a shoot in the mountains.

HOW EASY IS IT FOR YOU TO ESCAPE WORK?

James: Our weekends are often spent recovering from the previous week and then preparing for next one. Weekends work particularly well when our children come home—then it revolves around conversation and food. There's an inherent connection between food and groundedness.

IN YOUR INTRODUCTION TO (UK COMPOSER AND HOME COOK) ORLANDO GOUGH'S RECIPE JOURNAL, YOU TALK ABOUT HOME COOKING THAT NOURISHES "BOTH BODY AND SOUL." ARE TIMES WITH FAMILY AND FRIENDS AROUND A KITCHEN TABLE THE TIMES WHEN YOU FEEL MOST GROUNDED?

James: The best times are often with Orlando in the kitchen. I do really love the man. When he's cooking, there's always a lovely, relaxed conviviality, a great clattering of pans and much swearing. Once the food is there, though, you've got to pay attention.

DO YOU BOTH ENJOY COOKING?

Jessica: Buying, preparing, growing, cooking and eating food is something that binds all parts of our lives together.

James: Jess cooks very well. I cook but… laboriously. I make porridge.

Jessica: In many permutations… I get breakfast made for me. Then we switch to toast at weekend. We have it with homemade marmalade, either mine or Orlando's. Of course, we're both advocates for our own marmalade. Orlando and I often cook together.

James: I sit at the table and talk.

Jessica: We have glorious bonfire celebrations outside with friends. James makes a beautifully crafted fire. An open fire is instant calm. We even ripped our house apart for a full 18 months to gain an open fire in our drawing room. And of course, everyone always ends up in the kitchen—inside in the winter, or just outside in a seating area we have there. The reality of life is that those moments are rarer than they should be.

I suppose it's about creating easily accessible escapes. A couple of weekends ago, we put up a swing—an oak seat, lovely hemp rope. I loved the whole process, the knots and the spirit level. When we are away, I can see it hanging there—a symbol of escape. A swing gives such a sense of freedom and childlike enjoyment. Moments of play are important.

FOR MANY PEOPLE IN THE UK, LONG WEEKENDS IN TENTS AND CAMPER VANS AT FESTIVALS ARE AN ACCESSIBLE ESCAPE, A PLACE TO LET GO AND PLAY.

Jessica: Absolutely. It's possible to find true freedom there—when you arrive, you cast off daily life, responsibility, mobiles and ego—and slow down. There's no need to get in a car and drive. The day becomes free and open to drift around and find stimulation, peace or companionship. It's the mix of experience that festivals provide that hits the spot—something in the celebration of the arts and outdoors. It's an environment that's freer than a booked holiday. Often on holiday, you're still attached by a thread to daily life.

I suppose "glamping" [fancy camping] is symptomatic of the way we still want to experience something unique and different but less extravagant. But it's more than that, it's a way of beginning to explore unique ways to live—the mainstream is the bit that is falling away.

SO IS FINDING BALANCE ABOUT ESTABLISHING A KIND OF FLOW FROM ONE MOMENT TO THE NEXT, FROM WORK TO HOME, INSIDE TO OUTSIDE?

Jessica: If only life were like that! I guess I just try to make the most of work and home life, to appreciate all the gifts we're given. There is so much to be thankful for.

HOW DO YOU THINK YOU WILL SPEND WEEKENDS WHEN YOU RETIRE?

Jessica: I suppose, by then, there'll be no distinction. When you don't work, what's a weekend? You could take the moments for rest and relaxation when you need them. In an ideal world, that's how we should respond to life.

James: It's how we should be able to operate. Maybe the secrets lie in breaking the rules. But people like routine. Certainly some of the happiest times we've had have been those lunches with friends when we should have been working. ○○

Louisa Thomsen Brits is a writer, mother of four, tribal belly-dance teacher and novice coffee roaster. She lives in East Sussex, United Kingdom.

A WHOLE WEEK

WORDS BY REBECCA PARKER PAYNE & PHOTOGRAPH BY CARISSA GALLO

*Weekends are wonderful, but weekdays deserve some love too.
Let's face it: We live most of our lives during the week, so here are some
ideas for keeping those middays meaningful.*

Monday through Friday weigh heavy but Saturdays and Sundays are sweet respite, a burden lifted. On the weekends, hours dangle freedom from their hands like birds on a string. The freedom is sometimes gentle and swaying on the front porch rocker, and other times it's wild and raucous and dancing till dawn.

The rhythm of the week is a constant approach and recession. It pounds against our heads as we're tugged from our beds each morning. There is this duality, this dichotomy of worlds. We see the weekdays, the hard and the frustrating, and then we see the weekend, the reprieve, the transient oasis.

We're building lives with these days, and we can't sustain a duality where the weekdays are bad and the weekend is the only good. For our sake, there has to be more. We lament our time, and over the years, our attitudes turn from resilience to regret, duty to obligation. In the end, our divided lives decline toward bitterness.

The truth is, wherever you are and whatever you do, work is work. It's hard and rewarding but it does not end. So we must aim to cultivate wholeness to our days. We need to inhabit the weekdays with the same vigor and presence with which we embody the weekends—because we don't have to stay here where we regret our weekdays. There is joy to be had on Wednesdays just as much as Saturdays, but it requires a conscious choice.

Here are some tips for keeping your days full and alive regardless of where you stand in the week.

USE YOUR MORNINGS Get up early to catch the sun peek over the horizon. Put some music on, read your book or go for a run. Meet a friend for early morning conversation over coffee and scones. You feel like the day is yours when its starts as yours. Give yourself or your loved ones this time.

GO OUT See a concert or walk to your closest movie theater. Get cocktails before, and get dressed up. Make your nights something to look forward to, for gathering and experiencing culture and community.

INTENTIONALLY CULTIVATE BEAUTY A small amount of effort makes you feel like your time—even if it's a Tuesday morning—is something special, something worth remembering. So, stand over the French press as you smell the fresh grounds of coffee, fill vases with flowers on your desk and in your kitchen. Light candles when you wake up and leave notes for loved ones to discover later.

MAKE A BREAK When you get off work, go for a walk or throw open the windows and pour a glass of wine. Turn the stove on and invite the neighbors over for an impromptu dinner. Do the things that will bring you back into yourself, the self that seems distant at the end of a long workday. ○○

Rebecca Parker Payne is a writer from Virginia, where she bakes pies, drinks bourbon and spins old bluegrass on vinyl with her husband. She writes about all things concerning food, family, community and place.

THE AFTER-HOURS CHEF

WORDS BY ROMY ASH & PHOTOGRAPH BY CARISSA GALLO

Does living with a chef sound like a dream? Romy Ash lives with one, and she does most of the cooking at home.

"It must be wonderful," a new friend says. "What does he cook you?" "A cornucopia of gourmet delights," I reply, but I'm being sarcastic. In our home, I cook. When I first met my boyfriend, a chef by trade, I was under the same romantic misconception—that dating a chef would mean I'd always be served elaborate dinners on restaurant plates with a drizzle of *jus* around the edge.

Now that I'm not so naive, I've heard all the stories. After serving haute cuisine to diners, chefs finish work and on the way home pick up drive-through takeaway: greasy hamburgers, fries. They're exhausted, sometimes having been on their feet for 16 hours pulling back-to-back shifts, a norm in the restaurant industry.

If I want my boyfriend to cook me dinner, I book a table at his restaurant. Sometimes I go with friends, but sometimes I book a table for one. Eating dinner alone is something that must be done with complete confidence. I drink a glass of wine, and when my meal comes, it'll be off the menu, something a little special, made with care and love. But I never visit on the weekend, when the restaurant is at its busiest. He's been prepping all week, and the kitchen is too hot and high stress. On the weekends, I am absolutely independent, his job never allowing us to fall under the comfortable cloak that relationships often provide. Sometimes it's lonely.

When he arrives home from work, I'm usually asleep, but when I wake to say hello, what's most obvious is the scent of the kitchen he's just come from. Where he works now, they hand-cut chips. They are very good, thick, each one a little irregular, crispy on the outside and pillowy on the inside. When he leans down to kiss me, what I smell are these chips, the fryer. After a night at his previous job, he smelled more perfumed when he came home—a mix of quinces, of herbs and the smell of wine hitting a hot pan. That kitchen was small and French. When I first met him, it was a much richer scent, thick with spice, with chipotle, cumin and the smoke of charred meat. These kitchen scents are the restaurant's calling card.

On Mondays when I can work from home, we share brunch together. It's his Saturday, but I will have done half a day's work by the time he wakes. When he does, I'll make coffee, and in the time it takes for me to grind the beans and boil water, he has made me breakfast. He makes an omelet, whisking the eggs with a fork, pouring the eggs into a hot cast-iron pan, making a quick filling of herbs and goat cheese before folding the omelet over itself. It's just about the simplest thing, but the mark of a chef is the quality of their omelet. He butters me thick pieces of toast and we sit down to eat. When he holds my hand across the table, I can feel calluses in the shape of his favorite knife. We'll smile and break bread, crunch our toast, for a moment, content in the strange rhythm of a chef's nights and days. ○○

When Romy Ash is not writing about food, she writes fiction. Her debut novel, Floundering, *was released last year. She lives in Melbourne, Australia, where a cold wind often blows.*

OCT / 2013

SUN	MON	TUE	WED	THU	FRI	SAT
		1	2	3	4	5 ✕
6	7	8	9	10	11	12 ✕
13	14	15	16	17	18	19 ✕
20	21	22	23	24	25	26 ✕
27	28	29	30	31		

SEP / 2013

S	M	T	W	T	F	S
1	2	3	4	5	6	7
8	9	10	11	12	13	14
15	16	17	18	19	20	21
22	23	24	25	26	27	28
29	30					

NOV / 2013

S	M	T	W	T	F	S
					1	2
3	4	5	6	7	8	9
10	11	12	13	14	15	16
17	18	19	20	21	22	23
24	25	26	27	28	29	30

○ ....
○ ....
○ ....
○ ....
○ ....
○ ....
○ ....
○ ....
○ ....
○ ....
○ ....
○ ....

PROTECTING SATURDAY

WORDS BY AUSTIN SAILSBURY & PHOTOGRAPH BY JIM GOLDEN

We need weekends to restore, refresh and rejuvenate, but sometimes they end up being spent in super-stressful ways, taking care of errands or working. Our author explains his attempts to defend the weekend against outside threats.

We are living in the future. We're more technologically dependent, information hungry and intricately connected than any previous generation. We live and drive and date at warp speed. We are a people of the "ringtone," the "ping," the "like," the "poke" and the tweet. We upload, download, refresh, shareware and crowd-source. We are always consuming, connecting, working. Many have swapped privacy for connectivity. But there's one part of life that we won't surrender to the aggressive forces of "noise, news, now" in our house: We will fight to protect Saturday.

Living in Copenhagen, often regarded as one of the "happiest places on Earth," we know that we experience a relatively healthy work-life balance. We cycle to and from work, eat organic produce, enjoy several weeks of vacation time a year and usually have at least one workday a week with no evening commitments. We lead blessed but busy lives. But just like everyone else, we're susceptible to let both Friday's unfinished work and Sunday's commitments bleed into the one day a week when we don't *have to* work—the one day when we can go off-line.

For many people, Saturday is *the day* to reconnect with friends, pursue a group gathering or adventure or experience the crowds of their city. But for me and my wife, protecting Saturday means not only setting aside our digital devices but also pulling back from the many lovely people who populate the other days of our week. We believe that if we're going to be able to continuously nurture the precious friendship upon which our marriage is built, we need Saturday to slow down, work on being quiet and refocus on just being together. In this way, protecting one day for each other is both defensive and also chivalrous—a kind of "shining barrier" against the enemies of intimacy and intentionality.

So, what does protecting Saturday look like, you ask? Well, it can take a million different shapes, but a typical protected Saturday looks something like this... We wake up naturally—either the sun's light or the quiet whisper for coffee calls us from bed. Then we spend the morning watching the sailboats from the balcony and walking to the bakery for the greatest of all human pleasures: *les croissants au chocolate*. Then with Billie Holiday in the background, we spend the day reading, playing games, creating an extraordinary lunch and fading in and out of naps. If we're not properly dressed at this point in the day, chances are it's not going to happen, which, as you know, is splendid. In spring and summer, Saturday evening is all about making a dinner menu, executing it and then hunting down ice cream at the harbor. Autumn and winter evenings are more introverted, of course, as we make mulled wine and gather around the warmth of candlelight and our favorite old movies.

Whatever the season, protecting Saturday is about getting away without a plan—or making a plan and then completely ignoring it as we wallow in spontaneity and rest. On the best of these self-imposed Sabbath days, we sit together closer and for longer. We hear each other's words and silences better, and we rediscover the reasons we first found each other captivating. On protected Saturdays, we inhabit a private island, safe from the cares of the mainland and its 24-hour news cycle, with its relentless stream of updates and alerts and incoming messages. Once there, we're able to live out all the chapters of morning, noon and night as they naturally unfold. And there, on our island of protected days, we build upon the past, dream of the future and—perhaps most importantly—enjoy the subtle wonder of the present. ○○

Austin Sailsbury lives in Copenhagen, Denmark. He is currently at work on his first novel.

FEW

ENTERTAINING FOR A FEW

○ ○ ○

SURF & TURF

Some people seem to have perfected the art of mixing work and play.
Tokyo-based chef Shoichiro Aiba is one of them: Despite owning two
restaurants, he surfs, plays guitar and still puts his family first.
We chatted with him about how he makes it work.

WORDS BY JOANNA HAN & PHOTOGRAPHS BY HIDEAKI HAMADA
PRODUCED & TRANSLATED BY TINA MINAMI DHINGRA

Shoichiro Aiba is the owner and managing chef of Life, the popular Italian-Japanese restaurant in Yoyogi-Hachiman, Tokyo. He recently opened Life Son in neighboring Sangubashi, which serves "bread and mountain dishes" and shares a space with Tarui Bakery.

During his five years of culinary training in Florence and Tuscany (he sheepishly admits he moved to Italy after admiring a young Italian contestant on the show *Iron Chef*), Shoichiro learned not just how to cook well, but to live well. When he returned to Japan, the Italian cultural value of leisure and family time stayed with him.

In addition to running two small businesses, hosting community events, writing cookbooks and publishing his free local magazine, *Park Life*, Shoichiro is a surfer, photographer, musician, husband and father of two young children. We photographed him at home in Yoyogi, Tokyo, and at Ichinomiya Beach, Kujūkuri, Chiba, and interviewed him about his work-leisure balance.

HOW DO YOU MANAGE TO OPERATE YOUR BUSINESSES AND HAVE TIME FOR HOBBIES? ARE THERE EVEN ENOUGH HOURS IN THE DAY?

I've never felt that I needed more time. I dedicate 60 percent of my time to family and 40 percent toward work and my own interests. When my restaurant first opened, it was more like 90 percent work to 10 percent family. Work can take over life in many ways, but I intentionally and purposefully make an effort to meet with people and pursue my personal interests. Waiting until my "schedule clears" doesn't actually work, so I intentionally carve out my own time.

DESCRIBE YOUR IDEAL WEEKEND.

I'd wake up early, spend the morning being active and have a cup of coffee with friends. I'd then come home and share the happenings of the day with my family over a meal.

WHAT DOES YOUR ACTUAL WEEKEND LOOK LIKE? DO YOU HAVE THE LUXURY OF HAVING TWO CONSECUTIVE DAYS OFF?

I do. I've taken every Saturday and Sunday off since my son turned three. I don't work or surf on those days either—anything and everything I do then is with and for my family. We'll go to the park and play our hearts out. My entire weekend is for my kids.

WHAT IS LEISURE FOR YOU?

On my days off, I run, go on long drives, take naps in the park and regularly go surfing on my own. I've never, ever broken this routine—that's the trick. When I'm by myself reading my favorite book after I've gone surfing and start to nod off… sometimes I wake up and realize how relaxed I am— that's the moment I feel the most at peace.

Continued on page 74

THE NATURE OF YOUR WORK ALLOWS YOUR PERSONAL AND FAMILY LIVES TO INTEGRATE TOGETHER QUITE NATURALLY: DO YOU HAVE ANY TIPS FOR BALANCING WORK AND FAMILY LIFE FOR THOSE WHOSE JOBS DON'T ALLOW THEM THAT FREEDOM AND FLEXIBILITY?

Don't judge your life based on gains and losses. I always go with what feels best.

IN ITALY, YOU PICKED UP A WAY OF LIFE: "MAKE YOUR FAMILY YOUR FIRST PRIORITY, AND LEAVE YOUR WORK ON THE BACK BURNER." DO YOU FEEL YOU WOULD'VE ADOPTED THIS WAY OF THINKING IF YOU HADN'T LEFT JAPAN? HOW IS ITALY DIFFERENT FROM JAPAN IN THAT WAY?

I moved to Italy when I was 18, and it was my first time in the "real world." In Italy, everyone goes home during lunch breaks on weekdays. Many of the shops are closed on Sundays, and people take a month-long vacation in the summer. I thought this was an ideal way for people to live their lives. The Japanese in comparison tend to be overworked, but it's hard to compare the two since they're so culturally and environmentally different.

YOUR FATHER HAS BEEN A GREAT POSITIVE INFLUENCE ON YOU—FROM ENCOURAGING YOU TO SKIP COLLEGE AND TRAVEL ABROAD TO HELPING YOU MAKE IMPORTANT BUSINESS DECISIONS. WHAT HAS HE TAUGHT YOU ABOUT LEISURE? HOW DO YOU HOPE THAT YOU'RE SHAPING YOUR SON'S VIEW OF THE WORLD NOW?

Growing up, my father took me mountain climbing in Switzerland and exploring in Yellowstone National Park. The time I spent overseas significantly impacted who I am today. I wasn't able to readily accept everything my father suggested back then, but in hindsight I'm nothing but thankful for the environment he provided for his children. I want to also provide an organic and unforced environment for my kids. I'd like for them to take in as much of the world as they can, and the most important thing is to provide them with an environment that will make this possible.

AS SOMEONE WHOSE WORK IS TIED DIRECTLY TO FOOD, HOW DO YOU SEE THE RELATIONSHIP BETWEEN IT AND LEISURE? IS THERE A BOUNDARY BETWEEN THE TWO FOR YOU?

I consider food in two ways. The first is through the lens of what I do for work: I cook for my customer. The second is the relationship I have with food as a hobby and for my family. I'm lucky to be able to say that my hobby is to cook, and I cook for work.

IF THERE WERE AN EIGHTH DAY IN THE WEEK, HOW WOULD YOU SPEND IT?

I'm very much satisfied with how much I put into work and my hobbies, so I'd spend that extra day with my family. I certainly wouldn't mind having three-day weekends, though.

ANY LAST PIECE OF ADVICE YOU'D LIKE TO GIVE TO WORKAHOLICS?

Change your surroundings and your environment as quickly as possible. ○ ○ ○

Joanna Han is the assistant web editor at Kinfolk. *She lives, writes and drinks good coffee in Portland, Oregon, but is scheming to move to Sweden. Hideaki Hamada is a photographer based in Osaka, Japan.*

THE LIFE AQUATIC

"The cure for anything is salt water: sweat, tears or the sea," wrote Isak Dinesen. We couldn't agree more. Here are some ideas of things to eat and read as you set sail.

PHOTOGRAPHS BY CHRIS & SARAH RHOADS OF WE ARE THE RHOADS

"THE SEA"

A POEM BY BARRY CORNWALL
(1787–1874)

THE SEA! the sea! the open sea!
The blue, the fresh, the ever free!
Without a mark, without a bound,
It runneth the earth's wide regions round;
It plays with the clouds; it mocks the skies;
Or like a cradled creature lies.

I'm on the sea! I'm on the sea!
I am where I would ever be;
With the blue above, and the blue below,
And silence wheresoe'er I go;
If a storm should come and awake the deep,
What matter? *I* shall ride and sleep.
I love, O, how I love to ride
On the fierce, foaming, bursting tide,
When every mad wave drowns the moon
Or whistles aloft his tempest tune,
And tells how goeth the world below,
And why the sou'west blasts do blow.

I never was on the dull, tame shore,
But I lov'd the great sea more and more,
And backwards flew to her billowy breast,
Like a bird that seeketh its mother's nest;
And a mother she was, and is, to me;
For I was born on the open sea!
The waves were white, and red the morn,

In the noisy hour when I was born;
And the whale it whistled, the porpoise roll'd,
And the dolphins bared their backs of gold;
And never was heard such an outcry wild
As welcom'd to life the ocean-child!

I've liv'd since then, in calm and strife,
Full fifty summers, a sailor's life,
With wealth to spend and a power to range,
But never have sought nor sighed for change;
And Death, whenever he comes to me,
Shall come on the wild, unbounded sea!

GO, SAILOR

Sailing is an earned luxury, but it shouldn't require a six-figure paycheck or a yacht-club membership. The ocean can be enjoyed on a budget. Reward yourself for a week's worth of hard work by taking a day off and renting a boat. Luckily, there are organizations that make learning to sail both affordable and fun.

1. Contact local colleges and universities, which are great at helping wannabe sea captains get wind beneath their sails. If you ask nicely, many extend their offers to people outside of the college. Orange County Community College, for instance, hosts the School of Sailing and Seamanship, where you can learn to sail and rent boats at reasonable rates regardless of whether you are affiliated with the school.

2. Here in the Pacific Northwest, we have the Oregon Women's Sailing Association geared at helping the ladies get confidence in their skills. You can also check the American Sailing Association for info.

3. The most cost-effective option may be to become a short-term crew member through websites such as CrewFinders.com or WorkOnABoat.com. Joining a crew doesn't imply any level of seamanship—it provides an opportunity to trade a service like cooking or cleaning in return for time at sea and an opportunity to master the skills and gain licensure to sail.

4. We hear those famous group coupon companies also offer discounts on local activities like water-bound sports and dish out deals on sailing lessons and boat rentals.

5. Lastly, reach out on social media to find friends who know ways and places to sail. Don't head out on the seas alone—an experienced sea mate would be a handy guide.

Whether you opt to man the sails alone or take along a skipper, there is nothing more liberating than releasing the rope, paddling away from the dock and letting the wind catch in your sails. ○ ○ ○

We Are the Rhoads are Chris and Sarah Rhoads,
a husband-and-wife photography-directing team.
They like to travel the world, working in a
variety of environments.

Suggested sailing menu on the following spread.

SEA-SALTED COD

RECIPE BY MICHELLE DEBRUYN

This beautiful, simple recipe is perfect for a day on the water. The sea-salt shell seals in both moisture and flavor, and the fish is perfumed from the inside out while it bakes. While we tend to stick with fish that is in season, any mild, flaky whitefish is perfect for this recipe.

1 whole Pacific cod or other whitefish (about 4 pounds / 1.8 kilograms), scaled and cleaned

1 fennel bulb, sliced thin

5 sprigs of thyme

2 lemons, sliced thin plus additional lemons for serving

6 pounds (2.7 kilograms) course sea salt

METHOD Adjust an oven rack to the middle position and preheat the oven to 400°F/200°C. Rinse the fish, pat it dry and pack the cavity evenly with the fennel, thyme and lemon slices.

Pour half of the sea salt evenly into the bottom of a casserole dish large enough to fit the fish and arrange the fish on top. Cover the fish evenly with the remaining 3 pounds (1.35 kilograms) of salt and press firmly onto the fish.

Bake until a wooden skewer inserted in the center of the fish feels hot to the touch, 40 to 50 minutes. Transfer the casserole dish to a cooling rack. The salt will have formed a hard shell around the fish during baking, and should be cracked and removed before serving. Use the back of a spoon and sharply tap along the fish to do so. With a pastry brush, brush away any excess salt.

Once the salt shell has been removed, peel the fish's skin from cavity to the spine to reveal the perfectly tender meat. Squeeze a bit of lemon juice over the top, and dig in. We like this best served warm, but it's delicious cold, too. ○○○

Serves 4–6

OVEN-ROASTED CHICKPEAS

RECIPE BY MICHELLE DEBRUYN

A little bit salty, a little bit spicy, these roasted chickpeas are the perfect foil to the briny air of the sea. They crisp up nicely when baked, and the colors of autumn dust them just the way you've always dreamed. They're a snack, of course, but they're robust, and compliment a seaside meal just perfectly.

---

1 (15.5-ounce/440-gram) can chickpeas

1 tablespoon (.5 ounces/15 milliliters) olive oil

Salt

1/4 teaspoon paprika

1/4 teaspoon cayenne pepper

METHOD Adjust an oven rack to the middle position and preheat the oven to 425°F/220°C.

Line a rimmed baking sheet with parchment paper.

In a large sieve or colander, drain the chickpeas, rinse them and then drain them once more. Lay them on a clean kitchen towel and allow to rest until dry to the touch, about 30 minutes.

Transfer the chickpeas to a medium bowl and toss them with the oil, 1/4 teaspoon salt, paprika and cayenne. Turn the chickpeas on to the prepared baking sheet, and bake until the chickpeas are crunchy throughout, 45 to 55 minutes, stirring every 10 minutes.

Transfer the baking sheet to a cooling rack and allow them to cool completely, about 30 minutes. Eat immediately or store them in an airtight container for up to four days. ○ ○ ○

Makes a large snack for 2, or a standard snack for 4

THE
KINFOLK
TABLE

RECIPES *for* SMALL GATHERINGS

NATHAN WILLIAMS

INTRODUCING

THE KINFOLK TABLE:
RECIPES FOR SMALL GATHERINGS

BOOK DESIGN BY AMANDA JANE JONES

PHOTOGRAPHS BY PARKER FITZGERALD & LEO PATRONE

A look inside our very first cookbook

Food is the toffee-toasted mortar that binds people together, building stronger friendships that, when stacked sky high, create the most special of gatherings. Because of this, we're rather honored to announce the arrival of our very first cookbook, *The Kinfolk Table: Recipes for Small Gatherings*. Bringing together recipes, people and stories from around the world, we hope it'll encourage you to clink china with those around you and form new traditions to sit alongside the old.

Whether it's a neighborhood potluck, shucking fresh oysters or long days spent dipping lavender tea cakes into home-brewed coffee, the best soirées are based around camaraderie and community. Sometimes it's finding an unknown patch of dandelion root in your backyard that leads to spontaneous neighborhood brewing sessions, or spending the whole day searching for raspberries with your partner. To make it a complete experience, all you need is a friend or five to share it with. That is the culture of *The Kinfolk Table*.

The Kinfolk Table shines a culinary light on the creatives of Brooklyn, Copenhagen, Portland, Oregon, and the English countryside, inviting you into the lives and pantries of a diverse array of both enthusiasts and professionals, from coffee connoisseurs to ceramicists, fashion bloggers to florists, photographers to farmers and even an addition from one of our sweet retired grandmothers. These delegates from varying walks of life will provide you with inspiration for gatherings that begin as morning teas, drag into afternoon finger sandwiches and whirl all the way toward midnight pitchers of punch.

Entertaining looks different for each of us, but as long as we're cooking and inviting people into our homes with a genuine interest in connecting, conversing and eating together, then the way we do these things will ultimately come naturally. A burned dish or a missing serving piece becomes trivial. The humble soup or homely bread becomes a feast. It all seems quite simple.

WHAT IS *THE KINFOLK TABLE*? One-third cookbook, one-third narrative tale and one-third international adventure, *The Kinfolk Table* is a collection of 85 delectable recipes spread over nearly 400 pages from creative types around the world, set to inspire your next small gathering.

WHAT WILL WE FIND INSIDE? Inside the hardcover book, you will find a smattering of recipes from different cultures and backgrounds suitable for any time of day or occasion. Some of the suggestions are refreshingly simple, like throwing freshly plucked mussels on the barbecue or filling half a cantaloupe with yogurt and honey. Others may take a little more time and toe-tapping patience, such as Ginger Ice Cream with Kumquat Compote or perfecting a pot roast shoulder of veal. Danish, Japanese, Mexican and Korean influences make appearances too, as do fresh takes on classics such as Sweet Potato-Quinoa Burgers, Kimchi Couscous or Spiced Raw Chocolate Mousse.

WHO PARTICIPATED IN THE PROJECT? Each *Kinfolk Table* participant was asked to contribute because he or she lives a life consistent with the simplicity we try to promote in *Kinfolk*. Some of them are qualified foodsmiths, others just like making a post-hike brunch for their mates, but they all share one talent: a creative approach to their professional lives and an urge to craft a community based around a steaming pot of soup.

HOW DID YOU GATHER THESE STORIES? We traveled to every home featured in the cookbook to speak and eat with the makers. We sat at their tables and asked questions. We scribbled notes with lessons, tips and recipes. We left each of their homes with a big, cheesy grin of satisfaction on our faces and often stopped at the market for ingredients on the way home, empowered to cook each dish ourselves and share it at our own tables.

WHERE DID THE RECIPES COME FROM? The main cities we have chosen to focus on have been Brooklyn, Copenhagen, *Kinfolk*'s hometown of Portland, Oregon, and the English countryside. Of course, great food and even greater people extend beyond these borders, so we've added a "Wandering Table" section, featuring tales from Salt Lake City to family secrets from founder Nathan Williams' mother and grandmother back home in Alberta, Canada. In the future we hope to explore other neighborhood nooks and bring you more stories and recipes from the edges of the culinary world.

WHAT MAKES *THE KINFOLK TABLE* DIFFERENT? Instead of prompting you to purchase a kitchen utensil set the size of a small condo (or a fresh set of friends swanky enough to appreciate it), *The Kinfolk Table* puts the emphasis back into the relationships that surround eating, rather than the overly fussy details of entertaining. Let the people sharing butter around your dinner table be the foreground and superficial details such as fancy recipes and table decorations recede into the background.

For a special preview, you will find three recipes from *The Kinfolk Table* on the following pages to test out with your loved ones. ○ ○ ○

The Kinfolk Table: Recipes for Small Gatherings will be published by Artisan Books. It will be available in October 2013 wherever books are sold and at www.kinfolk.com.

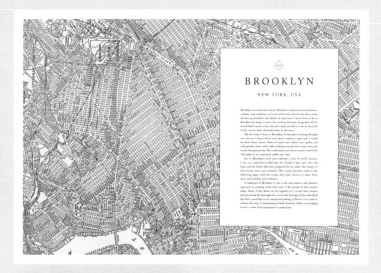

Wild Blueberry Currant Jam

Simple Market Vegetable Salad

FOR THE DRESSING

Whisk the vinegar, syrup, mustard, and lemon juice together in a small bowl. Slowly whisk in the olive oil and whisk until the mixture is emulsified. Season with salt and pepper to taste and refrigerate until needed. Whisk to reincorporate the ingredients before using.

FOR THE SALAD

Heat the olive oil in a small skillet over medium heat until shimmering. Add the walnuts and cook, stirring, for about 5 minutes or until toasted and fragrant. Season with salt and set aside.

Fill a medium bowl with equal parts ice cubes and cold water. Stir in the lemon juice and set aside.

Trim off the top and bottom ends of the grapefruit; the pink flesh should be visible. Set the grapefruit on a cutting board. With a sharp knife, cut the peel and pith off the grapefruit, starting at the top and working down the rounded sides all the way to the bottom. Trim off any pith pieces that may remain. Hold the grapefruit in the palm of your hand over a small bowl and carefully remove the segments by cutting into the flesh toward the center of the grapefruit, using the membranes to guide your cuts. (Alternatively, cut the peeled grapefruit crosswise into slices ¼ inch (0.65 centimeter) thick, then cut the slices in half.) Set aside.

Cut the stalk off the fennel bulb and discard, cut the bulb in half, cut out the tough core, and slice the bulb as thinly as possible on a mandoline (see Note). Place the slices in the prepared acidulated ice bath. Slice the radicchio as thinly as possible on a mandoline and refrigerate it in a salad bowl.

Slice the beet on the mandoline as thinly as possible and toss in the bowl with the vinaigrette.

Remove the fennel from the ice bath, pat it dry with paper towels, and add it to the salad bowl. Add the grapefruit and any accumulated juice and the parsley and toss to combine the ingredients. Season with salt and pepper and divide among four plates. Top the salads with the beets, walnuts, and thin shavings of pecorino cheese. Serve immediately.

Note: A mandoline is the most efficient tool for slicing vegetables paper-thin, as they should be for this recipe. If you don't have one, use a very sharp chef's knife.

Serves 4

BROOKLYN, NEW YORK, USA

Pulla
(Finnish Dessert Bread)

FOR THE DOUGH

1¾ ounces (50 grams)
fresh yeast

2 cups plus 2½ tablespoons
(500 milliliters) whole milk,
warmed to 95°F (35°C)

7 cups (35 ounces/1 kilogram)
all-purpose flour, plus additional
for dusting

1½ cups (10½ ounces/
300 grams) granulated sugar

1 tablespoon (5 grams)
cardamom seeds

1 teaspoon (6 grams) salt

12 tablespoons (6 ounces/
170 grams) unsalted butter,
softened

FOR THE FILLING

18 tablespoons (9 ounces/
255 grams) unsalted butter, at
room temperature

1 cup (7 ounces/200 grams)
granulated sugar

1 tablespoon plus 2 teaspoons
(15 grams) ground cinnamon

1 tablespoon (6 grams) freshly
ground cardamom

1 large egg, beaten

Pearl sugar

FOR THE DOUGH

Stir the yeast and milk together in a large bowl until the yeast is
completely dissolved.

Stir in the flour, sugar, cardamom and salt and mix until combined.
Stir in the butter. Knead the dough until elastic and slightly sticky,
about 15 minutes, by hand, 8 minutes with an electric mixer fitted
with the dough hook. Return the dough to the bowl, cover it with a
dish towel, and allow it to rise in a warm, draft-free place for 1 hour
or until it doubles in size.

FOR THE FILLING AND BAKING

Meanwhile, combine the butter, granulated sugar, cinnamon and
cardamom in a medium bowl and mix until thoroughly combined.

Lightly dust a clean, dry work surface with flour. Turn the risen
dough out and, with a floured rolling pin, roll it out into a 20-by-
16-inch (50-by-38-centimeter) rectangle about ¼ inch
(0.64 centimeter) thick. Spread the filling evenly over the dough,
reaching all the way to the edges, then, beginning with a long
side, roll the dough into a tight cylinder. Cut the cylinder into
16 triangles. Pick up the top point of the triangle and fold it
toward the center. Press the point tightly into the center.

Line two baking sheets with parchment paper and arrange eight
pulla on each sheet, spacing them about 2 inches (5 centimeters)
apart. Cover them with a clean dish towel and allow them to rise in a
warm, draft-free place for about 1 hour or until doubled in size.

Position two racks in the upper third and lower third of the oven
and preheat the oven to 400°F (204°C). Brush the pulla with the
beaten egg and sprinkle them with pearl sugar. Bake for 10 to
12 minutes or until golden brown and caramelized. Serve warm.

Makes 16 pulla

Hearty Barley Salad with Broiled Feta and Tomatoes

8 ounces (230 grams) feta cheese, cut into ¼-inch (0.64-centimeter) cubes

1½ cups (about 8 ounces/ 230 grams) small ripe tomatoes, such as San Marzano, halved

½ cup (about 2½ ounces/ 70 grams) pitted black olives, halved

¼ cup (0.4 ounce/10 grams) chopped fresh herbs such as oregano, rosemary and thyme

¼ cup (60 milliliters) extra-virgin olive oil

1 cup (7 ounces/200 grams) pearled barley

2 cups (475 milliliters) water

Salt

2 ripe avocados, cut into ½-inch (1.27-centimeter) cubes

16 ounces (455 grams) marinated artichokes, cut into wedges ½ inch (1.27 centimeters) thick

1 cucumber (about 8 ounces/ 230 grams), seeded and chopped

2 cups (2 ounces/60 grams) fresh basil leaves, thinly sliced

2 tablespoons (30 milliliters) fresh lemon juice

Freshly ground black pepper

NATHALIE: *The melted feta mixture serves as a hearty sauce for this salad. Feel free to customize it with whatever vegetables or herbs you like. Serve it warm with some good bread, maybe some charcuterie and good red wine.*

Position a rack in the center of the oven and preheat the oven to 392°F (200°C).

Combine the feta, tomatoes, olives, herbs and olive oil on a foil-lined baking sheet and toss until well mixed. Bake the mixture for about 25 minutes or until the feta has melted and the tomatoes are soft and brown.

Meanwhile, bring the barley, water and ½ teaspoon salt to a boil in a medium saucepan over medium-high heat. Reduce the heat to medium, cover, and simmer the barley for about 20 minutes or until it is tender. Fluff it with a fork and transfer it to a salad bowl.

Add the avocados, artichokes, cucumber, basil and lemon juice to the barley and toss to combine. Stir in the feta mixture. Season to taste with salt and pepper. Serve.

Serves 4

Almond-Jam Tart (Linzer Torte)

Adapted from Lillie's mother, Mary Etue Auld, who adapted it from a 1977 issue of *Sunset* magazine

9 tablespoons (4½ ounces/ 126 grams) unsalted butter, at room temperature

1¾ cups (8¾ ounces/250 grams) all-purpose flour

1¾ cups (7 ounces/200 grams) almond flour

½ teaspoon baking powder

½ teaspoon salt

⅔ cup (4.6 ounces/130 grams) sugar

1 large egg, at room temperature

½ teaspoon vanilla extract

¼ teaspoon almond extract

12 ounces (340 grams) high-quality raspberry jam

Sliced almonds

Coarse sugar

Confectioners' sugar

Position a rack in the center of the oven and preheat the oven to 350°F (177°C). Grease a 9-inch (23-centimeter) tart pan with a removable bottom with 1 tablespoon (14 grams) of the butter.

Combine the flour, almond flour, baking powder and salt in a medium bowl.

Beat the remaining 8 tablespoons (114 grams) butter and the sugar with an electric mixer on medium speed until light and fluffy, about 3 minutes. Scrape down the sides of the bowl with a rubber spatula, then add the egg and beat until fully incorporated. Add the vanilla and almond extracts and beat just until incorporated.

Press two-thirds of the dough into the bottom and up the sides of the tart pan. Spread the jam evenly over the dough.

Roll the remaining dough into a cylinder about 9 inches (23 centimeters) long and slice it into rounds ¼ inch (0.64 centimeter) thick. Arrange the rounds on top of the jam, slightly overlapping them, starting from the edge of the tart and working toward the center. Sprinkle the tart with the sliced almonds and coarse sugar.

Bake for 35 to 40 minutes or until the jam filling is bubbling and the dough rounds are lightly browned. Transfer the tart to a rack and cool completely, about 1 hour. Remove the tart from the pan, transfer it to a serving plate, and sift confectioners' sugar over it. Serve.

Serves 10

THE MILKY WAY

Does a couple whose media empire is built around the idea of family life get to have a life outside of work? It's tricky, but Milk *founders Isis-Colombe Combréas and Karel Balas discuss the way they live now.*

WORDS BY SARAH MOROZ & PHOTOGRAPHS BY KAREL BALAS

Milk magazine, founded by Isis-Colombe Combréas and Karel Balas, launched in Paris in September 2003. The mission was to showcase the contemporary family, addressing a readership of modern parents who take pleasure in "the culture of the visual."

"I wanted to look at family under my microscope," says Isis. "You can experiment on—or investigate—your family." For the founders, who are a couple and parents of two children, there's no boundary between work and leisure. All of it encompasses a coherent lifestyle that heralds the value of aesthetics.

The decision to launch a magazine was inspired by *Wallpaper* and the transversal nature of its coverage. "It discussed design, travel, lots of things," says Isis. "We realized a magazine could be a hybrid. But there was one thing it didn't discuss: being a parent. And I asked myself, why don't we discuss being parents? At the time, my little boy was five." (He is now 15; her daughter is nine.) So, at age 33, Isis left her career as a TV presenter to create the family brand with Karel (who was an art director for French publications such as *Jalouse* and *L'Officiel Homme*). Although Karel may have started off with more print experience, Isis has always been an opinionated sounding board.

"It's a clash all the time," she says of their decade-long professional relationship. "We're never in agreement on anything. It's a fight to have the power, aesthetically, so we make compromises. Creative duos are interesting. When you start losing your energy, the other brings new energy. It's harder to be creative alone."

Milk later loosened its initial family-focused mantra and launched an offshoot magazine called *Milk Decoration*, published quarterly, to reinstate its earlier purpose. "It talks about what I like to do: go to museums, explore flea markets, read novels," says Isis. "It's more culture than purely kids' fashion." Both publications celebrate the art of family life, knitting this concept together with the notion of esteemed French savoir faire and expertise.

"I felt that your family is your soundest investment, a source of inspiration," says Isis. "Your baby, the way you set the table. I had a lot of luck around me aesthetically: My husband comes from a family of painters and ceramicists." Surprisingly, Isis reveals that her upbringing was different from the vision and values she now embraces: She was raised on a hippie commune in Ibiza by parents who didn't believe in possessions and didn't own a house or checkbook, only coming to Paris later and adapting to urban life.

For the couple, the values of home and family get funneled into both the look and feel of the magazine. "Everything is chosen and selected. I seek beauty in every little moment," she says. "It doesn't always work, but I'm lucky when it does. A familial way of life is something that's worked at: it starts in the morning with what you listen to as you're making breakfast, what you eat—it's a whole. It's about the quality of relationships by way of aesthetics."

This aestheticism travels everywhere. "The only way to really break away from work is to leave Paris. The job doesn't end at 6 p.m. on Friday," Isis says. Thus, escapism becomes a deliberate choice: They go to the Île de Ré, an island five hours from Paris off the west coast of France, where the family has a second home. "The island is untamed," says Isis. "There are no advertisements in the village, and since we take photos for work all the time, it's nice to detox from that. The village is near the sea, and the kids can go wander off on their own since it's very safe and secure." The family rented a house there for years, then bought a residence in ruins that they completely overhauled. "For my husband, it's all about the kitchen," says Isis. "He cooks all the time. For me, it's about the flea markets and seeing friends, cycling, walking. We go once a month and for the whole month of August."

When they're not away at the island sanctuary, the family spends leisure time hunkering down at home. "We live in a calm neighborhood in the 14th arrondissement rather than in the trendy part of Paris," she says. "The weekend is about seeing photo exhibits or staying home and watching films. My husband goes to the market, and I do yoga or Pilates. We buy and read international press all the time. I love staying on the Rive Gauche, because it's calmer. I'm very happy to have our offices in the 1st arrondissement, near Colette, near the Louvre, with plenty of tourists. There's a real energy—it's the real Paris. But afterward, I need calm." ○○○

Sarah Moroz is a Franco-American journalist based in Paris. She writes for the New York Times *and* Monocle, *among others.*

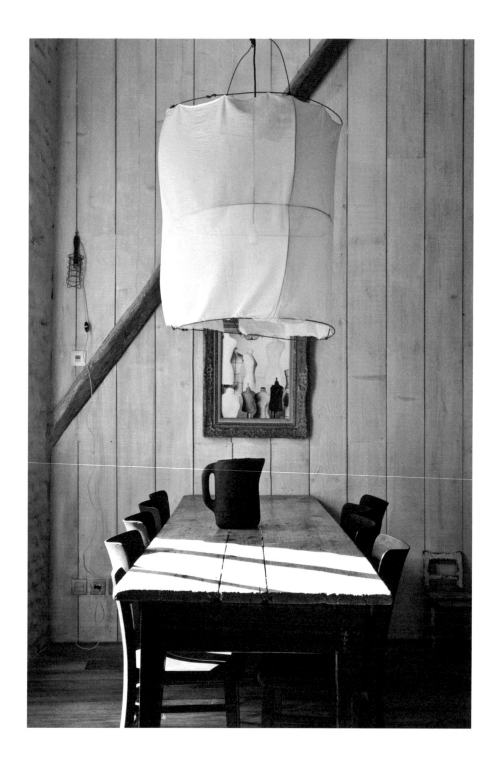

THE LAW OF THE LANES

COLLECTED BY GAIL O'HARA & PHOTOGRAPH BY PARKER FITZGERALD

Weekends are ideal for heading out on your bike. We asked some seasoned bike nerds for advice on how to stay alive on increasingly busy roads. (Our advice: Decorate yourself and your bike like a giant Christmas tree and use a megaphone.)

"Don't be a douche. No passing on the right. Use lights. Signal your turns. At the very least, slow way down at stop signs and look to see if there are any pedestrians."

JJ HELDMANN
SKIING MOM
PORTLAND, OREGON

—

1. Hands at 10 and 2.
2. Don't drink and drive.
3. Don't bogart the street or sidewalk.

TODD GFELLER
CARPENTER AND ROCKABILLY
MUSICIAN
DERRY, IRELAND

—

"Always stop at the lights because otherwise you'll hit a pedestrian or be hit by a lorry [truck]. Cyclists in London seem to have decided traffic lights are, at best, optional. And they've forgotten that pedestrians have dibs. As a bicyclist it behooves one to show a bit of respect for other people, I reckon."

ALEX MAYOR
MUSICIAN
LONDON, UNITED KINGDOM

"Make eye contact with pedestrians approaching you on the sidewalk, and if they look like they're going to blow a gasket, dismount until you've passed each other. In Vancouver, riding on the sidewalk is illegal, but people do it. It just seems polite and proper to visually check out the oncoming bipeds, to not make the sidewalk unpleasant for those who aren't up for the accelerated pace and drama."

JEAN SMITH
ARTIST AND MUSICIAN
VANCOUVER, CANADA

—

"Stop for pedestrians. It's okay to treat stop signs as yield signs, but actually stop if there's cross traffic. I like to pull to the left in a bike lane to let right-turning cars make a right on red. For God's sake, don't salmon."

RYAN OLSON
SOFTWARE DEVELOPER
LOS ANGELES

—

"The number one rule for me, the only one that matters really, is bike like you're in a car. That means own your piece of the road. Don't dawdle. Get off your phone. Signal. Don't swerve out in front of traffic. Wave thanks when people are courteous."

JIM KOURLAS
CHICAGO

"Assume you are invisible to cars and pedestrians. They'll never do anything to avoid killing you—because they cannot see you. It is solely your responsibility not to ever place yourself where a car or pedestrian could hit you. Ride completely offensively at all times."

ERIC WALLGREN
LABORATORY INSTRUMENT DESIGNER &
JOURNEYMAN PUNK-ROCK DRUMMER
WASHINGTON, D.C.

—

"Wear anything. Layers are good since you are going to warm up. Be careful with open-toed sandals or flip-flops. A 'skort,' combination of a skirt with shorts, can be good."

ROB SADOWSKY
EXECUTIVE DIRECTOR AT THE BICYCLE
TRANSPORTATION ALLIANCE
PORTLAND, OREGON

—

"Obey all traffic rules."

GREGG EINHORN
GRAPHIC DESIGNER
PORTLAND, OREGON

URBAN LOUNGING: A LESSON FROM THE DANES

Slappe *means* relax *in Danish, and we think these Copenhagen natives know how it should be done. Whether you're looking for places to nap, daydream, eat ice cream or read a great novel in the big city, here are some ideas for you.*

PHOTOGRAPHS BY ANDERS SCHONNEMAN & STYLING BY NATHALIE SCHWER

KICK BACK

Sitting on a bench alone seems like an egregious waste of space. When there's no one
around to share your seat with, take advantage of the momentary solitude by sprawling out,
shutting your eyes and enjoying a moment of peace in a bustling city.

GO OUT ON A LIMB

Trees grow in cities to remind us that outside the walls we build there are creations far
superior to the limits of man. So instead of reading on your concrete stoop this Sunday, put
on a fearless toddler-size grin, find some knobby branches and get climbing.

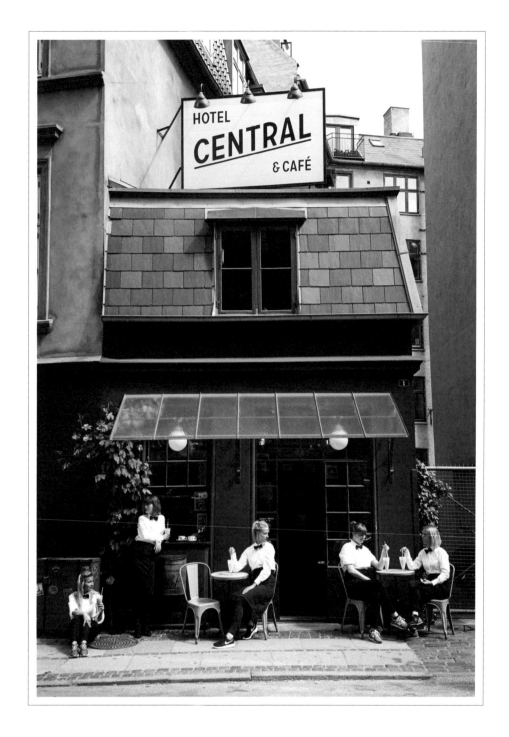

DRINK UP

Including coworkers in a post-shift beverage is a great way to forge more meaningful (and tasty)
relationships with the people you share a daily slog with. Make it a Friday afternoon tradition by
starting the weekend with a spiked milkshake, two straws to each parfait glass.

FIND THE WATER

Nothing clears your head like being near water. Walk along a canal. Take
a ferry connecting two cities. Even just parking yourself next to a big
fountain will help wash away your worries. ○○○

ROUTE: MILWAUKEE TO BROOKLYN

WORDS BY LIZ CLAYTON & PHOTOGRAPHS BY NICHOLAS MCELROY

Seasoned road-tripper and coffee/music writer Liz Clayton traces a familiar route in this issue's road trip guide. Grab a mixtape and ride along.

You've always wanted to see the Rust Belt. It's everything you thought it would be. From derelict industry lands to industrial dairyland, skipping along the northern roads to the Northeast has its extreme charms. Start in Milwaukee, the best small-scale big city the Midwest has to offer, and take in some art at the quite lovely Milwaukee Art Museum, or be thrifty and simply arrive at 10, noon or closing to watch its Calatrava wings expand or retract to the odd juxtaposition of canned-speaker music from outside. You could spend hours wandering the "antique" malls, restaurants, frozen-custard stands and dollar beer bars of this humble paradise, but if you do anything, make sure to spoil your trip to New York early with a stop at Jake's Deli. This historic Jewish deli on Milwaukee's North Avenue will seem at first like it's in the middle of nowhere—until you realize you've simply been waiting your whole life to arrive at this, its highest point. Order a Combo Reuben and a Cel-Ray soda, and enjoy the restaurant's recently extended hours (meaning you can go there after 3:00 p.m. on weekends!), worn-wood booths and impeccable meats. The haunting neon glow of the word "delicatessen" will beguile the rest of your miles, but don't turn back: You have a long way to go.

There's more to see and do in Chicago than you have time for, but those who fancy plants will want to spend some contemplative time at the Garfield Park Conservatory (and then head down to Little Village for tacos at La Chaparrita). Wish for a sunny day and azure lake on your drive along Lake Shore Drive, and head east. Whiz past the smokestacks of Northwestern Indiana and watch the land transform from steel mill to forest to breezy dune grasses: The quick stretch of coastline God gave Indiana to form the Indiana Dunes, full of quiet, endless-vista Lake Michigan beaches and clean sand.

Your departure via the Indiana Toll Road will be far from romantic, at least until you reach endless Ohio. Take in a quick survey of Ohio history told through the rest areas of the Ohio Turnpike, from the improbable Brady's Leap to the Battle of Fallen Timbers. Pull over in beautiful Cleveland for a drink (and perhaps a bite to eat) at the Great Lakes Brewing Company, a no-nonsense, fantastic craft brewery with nearly zero ambience and totally good soup. Admire the fact that neither the lake nor river are currently on fire.

Speaking of, Lake Erie gets a bad rap, and if you wish to seek out a view or two there are few better places to do so than from Pennsylvania's Presque Isle, just outside the strange throwback town of Erie, Pennsylvania. Cut down to Pittsburgh from here and partake of another of America's most handsome post-industrial cities: Brick streets and hilly neighborhoods line this open canvas of charm and promise. (Although if you're looking for something a little more *touristique*, definitely eat one of those deli sandwiches at Primanti Bros. where they put all those French fries on there.)

Leave the turnpike lifestyle from here and chug slowly toward Altoona: It's a long, bucolic slog on any route through this eternal state, and you may as well take the scenic route, or perhaps diverge along wrongly numbered highways such as the 85 brief miles of misplaced Interstate 99. Tiny towns such as Hershey and Birdsboro pepper this route of rolling hills, brilliant junk-tique markets and abandoned blast furnaces. Stop in Allentown for a trip to the Fairground Farmer's Market, used bookstores and a beautiful hamburger and glass of white birch beer on draft at Wert's.

Philadelphia makes a fine last pit stop, and a coffee (or wee tipple of beer) at Ultimo Coffee in Newbold/Point Breeze is a wonderful way to rejuvenate. Ignore the cheesesteak wars of Passyunk and nip up to Northeast Philly on your way out of town for a truly delicious sandwich at Joe's Steaks, formerly called something much more impolite, but with steaks that taste as delicious as ever.

And you've soon enough reached Brooklyn: Improbably great sunset vistas await you at East River State Park, or in, of course, Sunset Park. An endless menu of $14 cocktails or $3 egg creams beckons from myriad locations across the borough, sopped up by bagels unmatchable anywhere else—we like the Bagel Hole toward the south end of Park Slope. Take in the interior design histories of America depicted in room dioramas at the Brooklyn Museum and head down to Sheepshead Bay for a Roast Beef and Cheez Sandwich at the timelessly preserved Roll-n-Roaster. The servers aren't on roller skates anymore—but you'll feel like you are. You have arrived at the edge of the land (or almost—that's just a marina), and it's time to raise a crinkly fry to the memory of all the miles behind you. ○○○

Liz Clayton is a writer and photographer based in Brooklyn, New York. Her work has appeared in Serious Eats, The Globe and Mail *and* The Yo La Tengo Gazette. *She recently released* Nice Coffee Time, *a book of photographs from cafés and kitchens around the world.*

CHOCOLATE TOFFEE WALNUTS

WORDS BY ROMY ASH & SARAH TROTTER

PHOTOGRAPHS BY LAUREN BAMFORD & STYLING BY SARAH TROTTER

You don't want to be lost in the woods without proper snacks. These contain all the basic food groups: sweet, salty, crunchy and chewy.

Walnuts are at their best in the fall—fragrant, sweet and not bitter at all. Covered in toffee, dark chocolate and with a final layer of raw cacao, this treat is decadent. Bring them out in the late afternoon, when the sun gets so low, it's like you're racing it to the horizon. After driving all day, this treat can bring a car full of tired travelers back to full energy levels.

---

2 1/2 cups (10.5 ounces/300 grams) walnuts

1 cup (7 ounces/200 grams) caster or superfine sugar

1 tablespoon (.5 ounces/15 milliliters) water

10.5 ounces/300 grams couverture or dark cooking chocolate

1 teaspoon cocoa powder

METHOD You will need to work quickly when making this recipe, so it's important to have all the ingredients ready.

Arrange the walnuts in a single layer on a rimmed baking sheet. Bake them in an oven preheated to 350°F/180°C, stirring occasionally, until golden and fragrant, 12 to 15 minutes. Transfer baking sheet to a cooling rack and cool walnuts completely, about 20 minutes, prior to using.

Place the toasted walnuts in a bowl and lay out a sheet of baking paper on a work surface or baking sheet. Have a mat, tea towel or some silicone ready for your hot toffee pot, too.

Place the sugar and water in a dry, heavy-bottomed medium saucepan. Heat the mixture over low heat and cook, swirling the pot occasionally, until it turns pale golden and syrupy. Turn off the heat, add the walnuts and stir the mixture with a silicone spatula until the walnuts are completely coated. Everything will be extremely hot, so be careful.

With the spatula, scrape the mixture out in batches onto the prepared parchment paper. Don't panic if they stick together; you can always crack them apart when they cool. Set the candied walnuts aside to cool.

Bring a medium pot of water to a boil over high heat. Place the chocolate in a dry bowl that will fit over the pot. Reduce the heat to low and set the bowl over the pot, making sure the bottom doesn't touch the water. Stir the chocolate occasionally, until melted and glossy, taking care not to let any water or liquid into the bowl, as the chocolate will break.

Add the walnuts to the chocolate and stir until they're lightly coated. Spread out a new sheet of parchment paper and spread the nuts over it. Set aside to cool, preferably in a cold spot. Once the chocolate is set, break up the walnuts. Put your chocolate walnuts into a jar and add the cocoa powder, tossing to coat.

Note: To clean your toffee pan: run very hot water in the pan until the toffee melts and dissolves. ○○○

Makes about 2 1/2 cups

CRISPY HAM AND CORNMEAL WAFFLES

RECIPE & FOOD STYLING BY MARÍA DEL MAR SACASA
PHOTOGRAPH BY WILLIAM HEREFORD

Melting butter, orange-hued yolks from fresh eggs, bright yellow cornmeal, sizzling bits of thick-cut ham—these waffles are a tribute to the weekend.

Weekends provide solace and respite from the cluttered noise that we endure during the week. Blankets pulled tighter, loved ones gazed on more thoughtfully, clocks ignored. Coffee will be freshly ground, and its aroma deeply inhaled. We'll sprawl belly-down on the living room floor, still in our pajamas, and read that book that we were too exhausted for during the week. Best of all, the kitchen becomes a sanctuary, and food will be appreciated.

---

2 sticks (8 ounces/225 grams) unsalted butter, melted and slightly cooled

8 ounces (225 grams) ham, preferably country ham, chopped or shredded by hand

1 1/2 cups (7.5 ounces/210 grams) all-purpose flour

1/4 cup (1.25 ounces/35 grams) coarse yellow cornmeal

3 tablespoons (1.5 ounces/45 grams) granulated sugar

2 teaspoons (.2 ounces/6 grams) baking powder

1 1/2 teaspoons (.16 ounces/4.5 grams) baking soda

1/2 teaspoon (.1 ounce/3 grams) salt

2 large eggs

1 1/2 cups (12 ounces/350 milliliters) buttermilk

METHOD *Note:* Adjust one oven rack to the middle position and preheat the oven to 200°F/95°C.

Heat 1 tablespoon of the butter in a medium skillet over medium-high heat. Cook the ham, stirring occasionally, until well crisped, about five minutes. Remove from heat.

Heat waffle iron according to manufacturer's instructions.

In a large bowl, whisk together the flour, cornmeal, sugar, baking powder, baking soda and salt.

In a medium bowl, beat the eggs, then whisk in the buttermilk and remaining butter. Whisk the wet ingredients into the dry ingredients. Stir in the ham.

Cook the waffles and transfer them to the preheated oven to keep warm.

Serve with Sweet Pickled Peaches (see next page) and/or Whipped Butters (see page 136).

Make waffles up to one month in advance. Cool them completely and freeze them in zipper-top bags. Reheat the waffles in a toaster oven or an oven preheated to 300°F/150°C.

Notes: I use a standard waffle iron that makes one 7-inch round waffle. While you can use a Belgian waffle iron, the waffles won't be as crisp. You can, however, bake the thicker waffles in an oven preheated to 350°F/180°C until they crisp. Can be made without ham or with bacon instead. ○ ○ ○

Makes about 8 (7-inch/18-centimeter) waffles

QUICK PICKLED PEACHES

RECIPE & FOOD STYLING BY MARÍA DEL MAR SACASA
PHOTOGRAPH BY WILLIAM HEREFORD

*Although some things are best served simply with dollops of butter
and maple syrup, sugar-drenched fruit may help maintain a semblance
of a healthy breakfast.*

These pickled fruits should be eaten within one month of preparation and stored under refrigeration. If you want to store them for longer, be sure to follow proper procedures for canning.

---

4 ripe but firm peaches

*1 1/4 cups (10 ounces/300 milliliters)
apple cider vinegar*

1 cup (8 ounces/250 milliliters) water

1/4 cup (3 ounces/85 grams) honey

*2 tablespoons (1 ounce/30 grams)
granulated sugar*

Pinch salt

1 teaspoon whole allspice

1 teaspoon black peppercorns

1/2 teaspoon whole cloves

6 star anise pods

3 cinnamon sticks

METHOD Prepare an ice bath in a medium mixing bowl (enough ice and water to fill the bowl). Bring a medium pot of water to a boil over medium-high heat. With a paring knife, make a very shallow "x" at the bottom of each peach. Boil the peaches for 15 seconds and immediately transfer them to the ice bath with a slotted spoon. When cool enough to handle, remove and discard the peaches' skins.

With the same paring knife, cut wedges out of the peaches and discard the pits.
In the now empty saucepan, combine the vinegar, water, honey, sugar, salt and dried spices. Bring the mixture to a boil over medium-high heat, stirring until the honey and sugar are completely dissolved.

Distribute the peaches among one large or multiple medium glass containers or jars with lids and add enough of the hot pickling liquid to cover them. Cool, uncovered, to room temperature, then cover and refrigerate until ready to serve.

Note: Make this recipe year-round by using seasonal fruits, such as pears in the fall and quince in the winter. ○○○

(See three different recipes for Whipped Butter on page 136.)

THE UNEXPECTED SOIRÉE

We don't need a birthday or national holiday to set off fireworks or throw a party. We will make our own rituals and celebrate the time we've got for any old reason.

PHOTOGRAPHS BY RUPERT LAMONTAGNE & STUDIO GARÇON GARÇONNE

SATURDAY SLOG: A CAUTIONARY TALE

WORDS BY DAVID COGGINS & PHOTOGRAPH BY JUSTIN CHUNG

Is it possible to jog on the streets of the West Village without being seen, noticed or recognized? Our intrepid jogger makes his way to the local greenmarket and finds the answer is no.

After some months of emotional turmoil, I decided to jog Saturday mornings along Manhattan's West Side Highway. The fact that I use the word "jog" betrayed my novice status to a friend accustomed to hard-core training. "Does anybody jog anymore?" she asked with derision. Point taken. Yet what I do cannot technically be classified as running, after the persuasive opening dash from my apartment. This torrid pace lasts about a thousand yards before settling in a perfectly respectable pace for about 15 minutes. It then slows to the tragicomic for the final painful, wheezing five minutes.

Saturday mornings seemed like the most strategic time for my newfound outings. The West Village is not crowded, the streets freshly washed after the previous evening's vice. My virtuous morning doesn't end with my elaborate post-run walk-down, which is really the only part of the process I enjoy. No, I would continue, post-jog, to the Abingdon Square Greenmarket. Here, I would gather my micro-greens, free-range eggs and other natural hyphenated goods, cost be damned. I was living the self-satisfied New York life that most people can only dream of overpaying for.

And yet I didn't want to be recognized. This seemed safe on Saturday at 8:30 or 9 a.m., hours generally devoted to recovery—no girls waiting in line for some awful brunch, no weekend shoppers migrating into the boutiques enjoying favorable exchange rates. Who could I possibly run into? Well, five minutes after my first venture, I ran almost directly into my college girlfriend. Now happily married with children, she looked at me with warmth, slight confusion and a bit of alarm that I was not causing myself considerable health strain.

Without breaking stride, I made a hand gesture that indicated that I would call her, though it could have been interpreted that I was unable to speak and jog at the same time (which was probably the case anyway). At the greenmarket, the man who sells me mushrooms and greens asked me if I was all right. Perhaps my vigorous post-workout sheen was less a winning glow than an unsettling red. I assured him I was fine—never better in fact—and continued on my way. Unfortunately, in the next stall was an editor at *The New Yorker*. I would rather not run into an editor at *The New Yorker* while wearing shorts. It feels diminishing somehow, and I suspect she would agree.

Though my workout was over, I began to run the other direction carrying my bags—when I hadn't intended on running for at least another week. After escaping the market with the last of my dignity intact, I decided against a visit to the health food store, not wanting to subject them to my sweaty presence. Instead, I stopped into the wonderful Italian bakery on my street where I've been a regular since it opened a few years ago. They have a simple traditional roll called the Pan di Ramerino that has a wonderful savory bit of Rosemary.

The lovely Italian man looked at me after a moment and said, "Sorry, I didn't see you." I think he meant that he didn't recognize me in reddish hue. Oh, did I mention I was wearing a bandanna around my head? I hadn't felt the need to admit that to anybody who didn't ask. Yes: running clothes, the greenmarket, the virtuous life. Nobody said it would be easy. But, then again, nobody asked it to be. I'll be out there next week. Just don't wave if you recognize me. I'll deny everything. ○○○

WEEKEND LEMON CAKE

RECIPE BY SHOTA TASHIRO & PHOTOGRAPHS BY PARKER FITZGERALD
PRODUCED & TRANSLATED BY TINA MINAMI DHINGRA

Lemon cakes are associated with weekends in France. When children smell them baking, they get excited that a holiday may be coming soon. My recipe was inspired by one I learned from my mentor (Sébastien Bouillet).

FOR THE CAKE

8 large egg yolks

1 cup (7 ounces/200 grams) granulated sugar

Finely grated zest of 2 lemons

1/2 cup (4 ounces/115 grams) sour cream

1 cup (7 ounces/200 grams) cake flour

1 teaspoon (.1 ounce/3 grams) baking powder

4 tablespoons (2 ounces/ 57.5 grams) unsalted butter, melted and slightly cooled

FOR THE SYRUP

1 cup (8 ounces/250 milliliters) water

1/2 cup (3.5 ounces/100 grams) granulated sugar

4 teaspoons (1 ounce/30 grams) honey

Freshly squeezed juice from 2 lemons

4 teaspoons (.67 ounces/20 milliliters) rum

FOR THE GLAZE

1 cup (4 ounces/115 grams) confectioners' sugar

2 teaspoons freshly squeezed lemon juice

METHOD FOR THE CAKE Preheat the oven to 320°F/160°C. Grease and flour or lightly coat with baking spray a 9- by 5-inch (23- by 13-centimeter) baking pan. In a large bowl, whisk the egg yolks, sugar, sour cream and lemon zest until combined. Sift together the cake flour and baking powder, then stir into the egg-yolk mixture. For easier incorporation, transfer about 1/2 cup (2 ounces/ 60 milliliters) of the batter to a small bowl and stir in the melted butter thoroughly. Fold into cake mixture with spatula. Scrape the batter into the prepared pan and bake for 20 minutes, then decrease the oven temperature to 280°F/140°C and continue baking until a cake tester inserted in the center of the cake comes out clean, about 20 minutes longer. Transfer the cake pan to a cooling rack and cool completely, about 30 minutes.

FOR THE SYRUP While the cake cools, bring the water, sugar, honey, lemon juice and rum to a boil in a small saucepan over medium-high heat. Stir the mixture until it's completely dissolved. Remove the syrup from the heat and allow to cool completely.

To avoid a mess, set the cake (still on the cooling rack) on a rimmed baking sheet. Lightly poke the cake all over with a thin skewer and slowly drizzle the syrup evenly over it.

FOR THE GLAZE In a medium bowl, whisk together the confectioners' sugar and lemon juice until smooth. If too thick, add more lemon juice, 1/2 teaspoon at a time. Pour the glaze evenly over the syrup-soaked cake and allow to set.

Note: For a festive presentation, wrap the cake in your favorite paper and bring it to your weekend outing. ○○○

Makes one 9- by 5-inch (23- by 13-centimeter) cake

Design and type by Olivier Rielland Nadeau
Photographs by Rupert LaMontagne &
Studio Garçon Garçonne

MY EVER-CHANGING WEEKEND

WORDS BY AMY HEREFORD & PHOTOGRAPHS BY WILLIAM HEREFORD

For each year of our life we're given 52 weekends. As the number of candles on our cake increases, so does our experience of how we spend those restful two days. Through her son William's photographs, mother Amy reflects on the changes life has afforded her.

My first memory of the unfettered joy of weekends took place as a young child on my family's large West Virginia farm. Their work was close to the earth, close to the bone. Generations of women fed hardworking men and picked and canned. The farm held the scent of yeast rising and pickling spices entwined with memories of snapping sugar peas and fixing a mess of dandelion greens.

As a young woman, I gathered on weekends with friends in Virginia farmhouses adorned with wildflowers placed in blue Mason jars. We prepared quiches and cassoulet. We married in our mothers' white gowns with our long hair tied into knots with baby's breath and ribbons. We brides of the '80s said our vows with belief and set out with simple faith, Julia Child and *The Silver Palate Cookbook* as guides. We formalized our social lives with small, careful dinner parties. When children came along, gone was the spontaneous, replaced by naps and early bedtimes. But Martha Stewart showed us that we could be elegant and well turned-out, even while scrubbing floors.

At 36, I became a single mother. Weekends were no longer about gathering or entertaining, instead consisted of soccer games, sleepovers and angst-driven Sundays. Time was measured in the leaps and bounds of poster-board projects and broken arms. Memories were made on our Saturday hikes to Sugar Hollow with my two younger children needing a slower pace while the older boys raced ahead. The image of my older son dancing atop the slippery, moss-covered rocks of the waterfall is forever ingrained in my mind, reminding me that life is fleeting.

The meaning of a weekend evolves over the course of life. It shifts as we develop—learn to walk, ride a bike, kiss a boy, organize a dinner party, write a story, bid one's children farewell and then welcome them back, dreaming of grandkids in tow.

When the children left for college to pursue their dreams, my life became smaller. Learning to cook for one can be a hard, unforgiving process. Weekends became very long expanses of time, and how to use them became the question. An empty nest is not really empty. Instead, after children leave, time becomes about choosing what to keep, what to leave behind and what to explore more fully.

Now weekends provide the opportunity to stay put. Perhaps to plant a garden that I won't leave behind, pulling fresh beets from the earth to roast for the people I love. Music and beauty have become increasingly important—friends now sing for their supper and endure my reading of Mary Oliver poems praising the land and the kinship of friends. Having returned to my roots, I bid my children to join me for weekends close to earth. ○○○

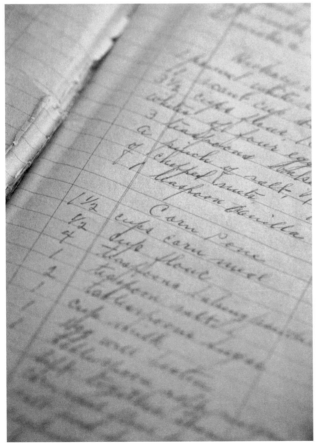

THREE WHIPPED BUTTERS

RECIPES BY MARÍA DEL MAR SACASA

SALTY HONEY BUTTER

2 sticks (8 ounces/225 grams)
unsalted butter, softened

6 tablespoons (4.5 ounces/125 grams) honey,
plus additional for drizzling

2 teaspoons (.4 ounces/12 grams) Maldon salt,
plus additional for sprinkling

METHOD Whip the butter, honey and salt with an electric mixer on medium speed or by hand with a whisk until all ingredients are combined and butter is fluffy, about two minutes. Transfer butter to serving vessel and serve with additional honey and Maldon salt if desired.

MAPLE PECAN BUTTER

2 sticks (8 ounces/225 grams)
unsalted butter, softened

1/2 cup (2 ounces/60 grams)
toasted pecans, chopped

1/4 cup (2 ounces/60 milliliters)
pure maple syrup

Pinch salt

METHOD Whip the butter, pecans, syrup and salt with an electric mixer on medium speed or by hand with a whisk until all ingredients are combined and butter is fluffy, about two minutes. Transfer butter to serving vessel and serve.

VANILLA BROWN SUGAR BUTTER

2 sticks (8 ounces/225 grams)
unsalted butter, softened

3 vanilla bean pods, paste scraped out

2 tablespoons (2 ounces/60 grams)
dark brown sugar

Pinch salt

METHOD Whip the butter, vanilla bean, brown sugar and salt with an electric mixer on medium speed or by hand with a whisk until all ingredients are combined and butter is fluffy, about two minutes. Transfer butter to serving vessel and serve.

Note: Use these butters on waffles or on pancakes, toast and fresh muffins. Butters may be wrapped in plastic and stored, refrigerated, for up to one month. ○ ○ ○

Each recipe makes 8 ounces (225 grams) whipped butter.

NIÇOISE SALAD ON A ROLL

RECIPE BY DAVID TANIS

Although crisp garlic toast is wonderful, sometimes you want the opposite of crisp, as in this Provençal sandwich, called *pan bagnat*. The aim here is to let the juicy interior meld with the bread a bit. It's like a soggy salad (divinely soggy, that is) on a kaiser roll. It can be pared down to contain only tomato, or built up to include roasted peppers, grilled eggplant—even some good canned tuna. Garlic, olive oil and red wine vinegar are the most important elements. A few anchovies and capers make a nice addition too. Take a basketful to the beach. By the time you get there, your sandwiches will be at their peak.

1 pound (450 grams) ripe tomatoes, in assorted colors if possible

Salt and pepper

2 garlic cloves, minced

2 anchovy fillets, rinsed and roughly chopped (optional)

1 teaspoon capers, rinsed

3 tablespoons (45 milliliters) extra virgin olive oil

2 teaspoons (10 milliliters) red wine vinegar

Pinch of red pepper flakes

12 basil leaves

4 French rolls or a baguette, split

A few tender parsley leaves

Olive Relish (recipe in One Good Dish)

METHOD Cut larger tomatoes into thick slices or wedges and smaller ones into halves. Put them in a bowl and season with salt and pepper. Add the garlic, anchovies, if using, capers, olive oil, vinegar, pepper flakes and half the basil, torn or chopped. Gently toss with the tomatoes and leave for 5 to 10 minutes.

Spoon the tomato salad and its juices onto the bottoms of the rolls (or bottom half of the baguette). Lay the remaining basil leaves and the parsley over the tomatoes. Add a spoonful of olive relish to each roll (or 4 spoonfuls to the baguette), if desired. Replace the top(s) and press lightly. If using a baguette, cut into 4 pieces. Cover the sandwiches with a clean dish towel and wait for an hour or so before serving. ○○○

Serves 4

This recipe is from David Tanis' cookbook, One Good Dish *(Artisan Books), out in October 2013.*

SPECIAL THANKS
Paintings Katie Stratton
Partnership with Kodak

Kodak
PROFESSIONAL Products

ON THE COVER
Photograph by Hideaki Hamada
Photograph is of Shoichiro Aiba, owner and chef of Life
and Life Son. Shot on location in Yoyogi, Tokyo, and
Ichinomiya beach, Kujūkuri, Chiba, Japan.

THE WATER WITHIN
Styling Kristin Lane

WEEKEND INDULGENCES
Styling Kristin Lane
Special thanks to those who contributed product ideas
and sourced items for this story: Olivia Rae James,
Rebecca Parker Payne, Diana Yen, Danica van de Velde,
Karen Mordechai, Carissa Gallo, Julie Pointer, Joanna
Han, Adriana Jaime and the *Kinfolk* Team.

THE AFTER-HOURS CHEF
Styling Jen Vitale

PROTECTING SATURDAY
Styling Kristin Lane

SURF & TURF
Production & Translation Tina Minami Dhingra

THE LIFE AQUATIC
Direction & Photography Chris and Sarah Rhoads
Wardrobe & Prop Stylist Lisa Moir
Food Styling Michelle DeBruyn
Cinematography Caleb Babcock & Sean Lowe
Models Jonathan Mooney, Sydney Babcock, Zach Urban
Hair and Makeup Tricia Turner
Photo Assistant Matti Schumacher
Boats rented from the Center for Wooden Boats, Seattle

THE LIFE AQUATIC: SAILING TIPS
Thanks to Jodi Murphy, Taylor Stark,
Aubree Bernier-Clarke and Melanie English

THE KINFOLK TABLE:
RECIPES FOR SMALL GATHERINGS
Photographs by Parker Fitzgerald & Leo Patrone
Book design by Amanda Jane Jones

THE LAW OF THE LANES
Styling Riley Messina

RECIPES: CRISPY HAM AND CORNMEAL
WAFFLES, SWEET PICKLED PEACHES AND
THREE WHIPPED BUTTERS
Prop Styling Michelle Wong

THE UNEXPECTED SOIRÉE
Art Director Danny Demers
Creative Producer Diane Garcia
Models Daouda Ka, Ruben Bedeleem,
Anna Tao and Yollie

RECIPE: WEEKEND LEMON CAKE
Production & Translation Tina Minami Dhingra
Styling Riley Messina
Patissier Shota Tashiro
Paper design Czar (Ends and Means)

WORK LESS, REST MORE
Studio Garçon Garçonne
Creative Director Danny Demers
Creative Producer Diane Garcia
Art Director Anita Feng
Designer & Typographer Olivier Rielland Nadeau
Photographs Rupert LaMontagne

—

ENDNOTES

THE LIFE AQUATIC
The quote from Isak Dinesen (1885–1962), found on
goodreads.com, is from the book *Seven Gothic Tales*,
originally published in 1934 (New York: Vintage/
Random House, Inc., 1991).

This version of "The Sea" by Barry Cornwall was
chosen from bartleby.com. *A Victorian Anthology,
1837–1895.* Cambridge: Riverside Press, 1895;
bartleby.com, 2003.

On-line Published April 2003 by bartleby.com.
Copyright Bartleby.com, Inc. *Author* Stedman,
Edmund Clarence, 1833–1908. *Title* A Victorian
Anthology, 1837–1895; selections illustrating the
editor's critical review of British poetry in the reign
of Victoria, edited by Edmund Clarence Stedman.
Published Cambridge Riverside Press, 1895. *Citation*
Stedman, Edmund Clarence, ed.

WWW.KINFOLK.COM

KEEP IN TOUCH